Services Trade Policies and the Global Economy

This work is published under the responsibility of the Secretary-General of the OECD. The opinions expressed and arguments employed herein do not necessarily reflect the official views of the OECD member countries.

This document and any map included herein are without prejudice to the status of or sovereignty over any territory, to the delimitation of international frontiers and boundaries and to the name of any territory, city or area.

Please cite this publication as:
OECD (2017), *Services Trade Policies and the Global Economy*, OECD Publishing, Paris.
http://dx.doi.org/10.1787/9789264275232-en

ISBN 978-92-64-27492-1 (print)
ISBN 978-92-64-27523-2 (PDF)
ISBN 978-92-64-27527-0 (ePub)

The statistical data for Israel are supplied by and under the responsibility of the relevant Israeli authorities. The use of such data by the OECD is without prejudice to the status of the Golan Heights, East Jerusalem and Israeli settlements in the West Bank under the terms of international law.

Photo credits: Cover Illustration © Jeffrey Fisher.

Corrigenda to OECD publications may be found on line at: *www.oecd.org/about/publishing/corrigenda.htm*.

Foreword

This book synthesises recent work by the OECD on recording, quantifying and analysing services trade policies and their impacts on imports and exports, the performance of manufacturing and services sectors, and how services trade restrictions influence the decisions and outcomes of firms engaged in international markets.

Launched in 2014, the OECD Services Trade Restrictiveness Index (STRI) is a unique, evidence-based tool that provides information on regulations affecting trade in services in 22 sectors across the 35 OECD countries and Brazil, the People's Republic of China, Colombia, Costa Rica, India, Indonesia, Lithuania, the Russian Federation and South Africa. These countries and sectors represent over 80% of global trade in services. The STRI provides comprehensive, comparable data and benchmarks relative to global best practices.

The STRI database (http://oe.cd/stri), compiling requirements to enter foreign markets in unprecedented detail, provides transparent and readily accessible insights into the restrictions on foreign entry and the movement of people, barriers to competition, regulatory transparency and other discriminatory measures that hamper services trade. It is, therefore, an important reference for exporters and international services providers and a source of data for academic research on drivers and impediments to services trade.

The new evidence presented in this book is meant to inform trade policy makers about the likely effects of unilateral or concerted regulatory reforms and help prioritise policy action. The OECD's quantification of applied sectoral regulatory regimes, across countries and over time, has opened up new avenues for the analysis of services trade policy – a field that has long suffered from a scarcity of comparable data and indicators.

Taken together, the main findings and key recommendations of this work suggest that national administrations should consider adopting whole-of-government strategies to capitalise on the demonstrated potential of co-ordinated services trade policy and regulatory reforms to help make globalisation work for all. We hope that you find this publication and the STRI tools a useful resource in your quest for a better understanding of services trade, the role of services in global value chains and the policies that shape services markets.

Acknowledgements

The work that this book draws on was prepared under the aegis of the OECD Trade Committee with inputs from its Working Party. Delegates and observers contributed significantly through their verification of or comments to the Services Trade Restrictiveness Index (STRI) database and its updates for 2015 and 2016 and by discussions of the underlying work synthesised in this book. The assistance of the National Bank of Belgium, Statistics Finland, the Research Data and Service Centre of the Deutsche Bundesbank, Bank of Italy, the UK Office of National Statistics, the US Bureau of Economic Analysis, and Japan Ministry of Economy in analysing micro data is gratefully acknowledged. Magnus Lodefalk's help on analysing Swedish micro data is gratefully acknowledged.

The book was prepared by Hildegunn Kyvik Nordås, Dorothée Rouzet, Sebastian Benz, Janos Ferencz, Frederic Gonzales, Massimo Geloso Grosso, Sébastien Miroudot, and Francesca Spinelli under the supervision of John Drummond. Alison Burrell provided assistance in editing the book and Michèle Patterson supervised the publication process.

The authors would like to thank Ken Ash, Carmel Cahill, and Bernard Hoekman for useful comments and suggestions, and Kaveri Bopiah for research assistance on case studies.

Table of contents

Figures

Follow OECD Publications on:

http://twitter.com/OECD_Pubs

http://www.facebook.com/OECDPublications

http://www.linkedin.com/groups/OECD-Publications-4645871

http://www.youtube.com/oecdilibrary

http://www.oecd.org/oecddirect/

Acronyms and glossary

APEC	Asia-Pacific Economic Cooperation
B2B	Business to business
FDI	Foreign direct investment
FTA	Free trade agreement
GPA	Government procurement agreement
GVC	Global value chain
ICT	Information and communications technology
IoT	Internet of things
IPR	Intellectual property rights
IPTV	Internet Protocol Television
IT	Information technology
KIBS	Knowledge-intensive business services
KLEMS	EU project analysing capital (K), labour (L), energy (E), materials (M) and service (S) inputs on a detailed activity level
MNE	Multinational enterprise
MSMEs	Medium small and micro-enterprises
OTT	"Over the top"; an OTT service involves content, a service or an application that is provided to the end user over the open Internet
PSA	Personal services automation
SMEs	Small and medium sized enterprises
TFP	Total factor productivity

Executive summary

Services generate more than two-thirds of global gross domestic product (GDP), attract over three-quarters of foreign direct investment (FDI) in advanced economies, employ the most workers, and create most new jobs globally. Impediments to global services trade, however, remain pervasive as national trade and regulatory policies in individual services sectors are often made with limited regard for economy-wide impacts.

This book synthesises recent work by the OECD that analyses services trade policies and quantifies their impacts on imports and exports, the performance of manufacturing and services sectors, and how services trade restrictions influence the decisions and outcomes of firms engaged in international markets. The main implications emerging from the analysis highlight the magnitude, nature and impact of the costs entailed by restrictive services trade policies.

Main findings

Open and well-regulated services markets help make globalisation work for all

Dynamic markets with a thriving entrepreneurial spirit are an important factor in ensuring that economic growth is inclusive. Such conditions rely on global access to the networks, goods and services that carry knowledge around the world.

Open services markets are the gateway to global value chains

Open and well-regulated services markets ensure access to information, skills, technology, funding and markets in a modern, increasingly digital economy. Intermediate services reduce costs, improve quality, and match suppliers and customers around the world. Moving up the value chain, therefore, depends on a local business services sector open to ideas, skills and investment from cutting edge firms wherever they may be found.

Services reforms boost SMEs

It is clear that the cost of services trade restrictions falls disproportionally on small and medium sized enterprises (SMEs). In addition, regulatory co-operation to minimise duplication of compliance costs and better use of technology to ease the burden of administrative procedures would help SMEs.

Regulatory co-operation reduces trade frictions

Regulatory heterogeneity has a negative impact on services trade flows, over and above the impact of services trade restrictions. Conversely, countries trade more with partners with similar regulation. Trade agreements are likely to have the largest effect on trade when they, *inter alia*, reduce the level of trade restrictiveness hand-in-hand with forward-looking regulatory co-operation.

Trade in services depends on the movement of professionals

Cross-border movement of people may not account for a large share of services trade, but it is essential for international business operations. Mobility of natural persons across international borders is crucial, particularly for trade in business services, which in turn is an important channel for knowledge transfer.

Trade in services underpins the digital economy

Liberalisation and pro-competitive reforms in the telecommunications sector are associated with a substantial reduction in the trade costs for business services. High capacity networks at competitive prices are a necessary condition for a digital transformation of knowledge-intensive services. Access to the professions and the services they provide is also essential.

Trade-relevant regulations should keep up with the digital economy

A precondition for a dynamic market is that dominant firms cannot abuse their market power with impunity. In recent years, the start-up rate of new firms has slowed down considerably while market concentration has increased significantly. The best way of enhancing entrepreneurship is to ensure open markets with low barriers to entry for both local and foreign enterprises and entrepreneurs.

Key policy recommendations

- There is substantial scope for reducing trade costs in major services sectors by scaling back measures that discriminate against foreign providers. The largest gains would occur if domestic regulation regarding competition and transparency is concurrently improved.

- Regulatory co-operation makes doing business easier for exporters. Where high restrictions to services trade still prevail, reducing them remains a prerequisite for regulatory cooperation to make a substantial difference.

- Smaller and less experienced exporters face a steeper cost burden in more restrictive regulatory environments. Opening up services markets would primarily benefit SMEs, which are responsible for the majority of new job creation.

- The business models for supplying services are complex, often involving a combination of modes, a bundle of goods and services, or a mix of digital products and face-to-face interaction. In order to avoid distorting these business models, a balanced approach should be taken towards the different modes of supply across the spectrum of trade, investment and competition policies.

- There is not one service industry, but many services with different business models, competition challenges and best practice regulatory frameworks. To maximise the benefits of reform, targeted policy advice needs to identify the main bottlenecks by taking into account the level of actionable trade costs in each sector, how far sectoral regulation diverges from that of key trade partners as well as flow-on effects on downstream segments of the economy.

- Reforming services trade brings benefits for consumers and strengthens domestic productivity and economic performance. Modern manufacturing is a heavy user of high-tech services inputs and its competitiveness relies on access to state-of-the-art suppliers at the best price. Furthermore, countries with more favourable and transparent regulatory environments are also more attractive for FDI, which stimulates extra activity, jobs and exports.

Chapter 1

The rise of services in the global economy

Chapter 1 assesses the importance of the services sector within the overall economy. It discusses the role of services in recent macroeconomic outcomes, as well as the marked trend towards manufacturing becoming increasingly services-dependent. The chapter highlights some important megatrends, particularly the digital economy, which is largely supported by the services sector, and discusses the role of establishing appropriate services regulations in order to leverage the digital revolution to strengthen productivity. In light of the significant role that small and medium sized enterprises (SMEs) play in the economies of most countries, it considers policies in the services field that can facilitate their international development, both through internet platforms and enhanced participation in global value chains (GVCs).

The structural transformation towards services

Economic development is associated with a shift from an agrarian economy dominated by subsistence farming to an industrialised economy dominated by services. Figure 1.1 shows that the services share of GDP has increased over time across all country groups, with the fastest rise in middle-income countries. Furthermore, at any point in time the services share is on average higher the richer the country is.

Figure 1.1. **Services share of GDP**

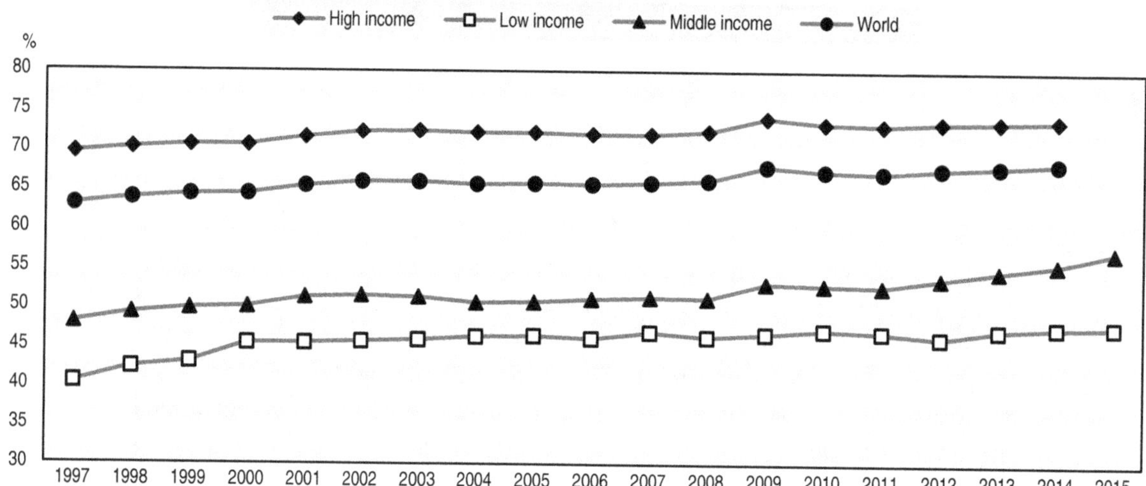

Source: World Bank, WDI.

The counterpart of a rising services share is a declining share of manufacturing and primary sectors in global GDP. The rising share of services and the corresponding decline in the share of manufacturing can be explained by faster technical development in manufacturing than in services, a shift in demand from manufactured products to services with rising income levels, and falling relative prices of manufactures. At the same time, in absolute terms output from both agriculture and manufacturing continues to grow steadily. For example, while the share of manufacturing in world nominal GDP declined from 20% in 1997 to 15% in 2015, the absolute level of global manufacturing output expanded by 44%.[1]

Structural changes in employment follow a similar pattern to those in industrial structure, as illustrated in Figure 1.2. It presents structural movements in employment for high- and middle-income countries during the period 1994-2010, and also for the People's Republic of China (hereafter "China") and India separately. The most significant reallocations in recent years have been in middle-income countries, where rapid urbanisation has drawn people from agriculture to urban jobs in industry and services. Comparing China and India uncovers a paradox. Over the 15-year period, China has become the manufacturing hub of the world while India has turned into a leading services exporter. Yet the services share in total employment rose twice as fast as the share of industry in China, while the opposite is true in India. Furthermore, the services share in total employment is much higher in China than it is in India. The explanation for this is three-fold. The transition from an agrarian economy is further advanced in China than in India. Thus, the share of agriculture declined from about half to about a third of total employment in China, while half of India's labour force is still in agriculture. Second, India has seen an unprecedented spurt in labour productivity in export-oriented services (Benz et al., 2017). Third, a supporting services sector has been an essential but largely overlooked part of China's industrial development.

Figure 1.2. **Employment by sector group and two country groups, plus China and India**

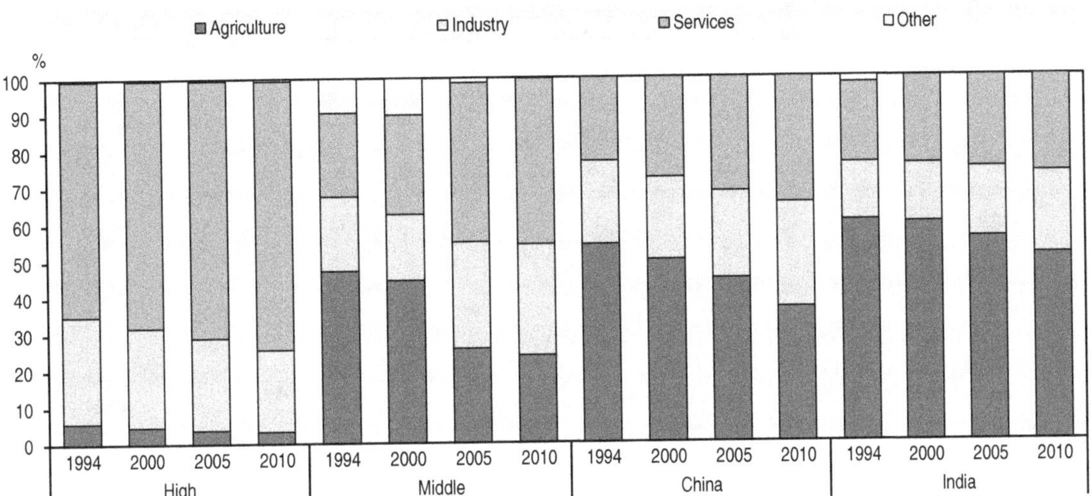

Source: World Bank WDI and Statistical Yearbook for China.

The structural shifts depicted in Figures 1.1 and 1.2 reveal that globally the share of employment in services has increased faster than the share of services in nominal GDP, which means that on average labour productivity has grown faster in manufacturing than in services. This has raised concerns that services-intensive economies may be less dynamic and create relatively fewer secure and well-paying jobs compared to the heyday of manufacturing employment. Such worries have led to a debate on a possible revival of classical industrial policy as a means of fostering an industrial renaissance accompanied by good jobs for low- and medium-skilled workers. However, the driving force behind a recent slow-down in offshoring and the trickling back of manufacturing to high-income countries appears to be precisely the diminishing importance of labour costs as the fourth industrial revolution unfolds.

The fourth industrial revolution is characterised by computer-integrated manufacturing, additive manufacturing, automation and advanced analytics of Big Data and the flow of information over the Internet of Things (IoT). During this transition, high-skilled manufacturing employment has been maintained both in high- and middle-income countries while low-skilled manufacturing employment has plunged (Rodrik, 2016). Judging from such trends, the employment share in services is likely to climb until it levels off at around 80-85%, while high-skilled jobs in manufacturing may continue to show resilience to technical changes. Like structural changes in the past, the ongoing transformation has immense potential for improving human well-being if managed wisely.[2]

Modern services are catching up with manufacturing productivity levels

The main driver of economic growth is a rising level of productivity. It is true that on average the level of productivity is higher in manufacturing than in services, but modern services are rapidly catching up. Table 1.1 presents recent developments in productivity for selected sectors in four countries.[3] At least one services sector has experienced faster productivity growth than manufacturing in all four countries. It is notable that wholesale and retail trade has undergone a higher rate of productivity growth than manufacturing in three of the four countries in recent years. This is a labour-intensive sector that has been among the early adopters of productivity-enhancing ICT in bricks-and-mortar retail and is currently migrating to digital platforms.[4]

Table 1.1. **Productivity (TFP) by sector, 2014**
Index, 2010 = 100

ISIC 4	Sector	United Kingdom	France	Germany	Finland
C	Total manufacturing	101.57	103.68	106.53	97.43
G	Wholesale and retail trade; repair of motor vehicles and motorcycles	104.26	104.02	105.40	98.62
H	Transportation and storage	105.74	97.37	94.56	113.40
J	Information and communication	98.17	103.98	116.35	117.45
58-60	Publishing, audio-visual and broadcasting activities	105.28	94.92	106.35	88.23
61	Telecommunications	92.87	123.58	106.75	142.75
62-63	IT and other information services	96.40	97.93	127.27	120.12
K	Financial and insurance activities	86.99	103.34	105.21	103.82
M-N	Professional, scientific, technical, administrative and support service activities	109.33	95.14	98.20	95.35
R-S	Arts, entertainment, recreation and other service activities	102.75	91.88	97.00	89.79

Source: EU KLEMS database, *www.euklems.net/*.

The professional, technical and other business services covered under ISIC codes M-N are a strong source of job creation for skilled workers and, with the exception of Germany, employ more people than manufacturing does. In this sector, productivity has kept up with manufacturing only in the United Kingdom. However, the digital transformation of professional services is still in its infancy with the promise of substantial productivity growth in the future. Furthermore, a number of studies have found that knowledge-intensive business services (KIBS) stimulate innovation and productivity in their client firms, including manufacturers. KIBS are typically coproduced with clients and their impact on productivity may be more visible at the aggregate economy level than in the KIBS sector.[5]

Comparable information on total factor productivity for emerging market economies is not readily available, but the WORLD-KLEMS database contains such information for India covering the period 1980-2008/9. Interestingly, TFP growth in services by far outperformed that in manufacturing in TFP growth in India during this period. Taking 1990 levels as the benchmark, the best-performing manufacturing sector (non-metallic mineral products) raised TFP by about 40%, while in the best-performing services sector (post and telecommunications) productivity grew six-fold over the three decades covered. India has embarked on a services export-led growth path no less impressive than previous growth spurts experienced by newly industrialised countries in the past. The experience of India and China, together with observations from de-industrialising high-income countries, suggests that an export-oriented services sector is possible even in the absence of a significant industrial base, while an export-oriented industrial sector without supporting services is unlikely.

Services enhance productivity and competitiveness in manufacturing

Services provide essential inputs to goods-producing sectors, enhancing productivity or competitiveness or both. Education and health contribute to raising the skill levels and adaptability of workers. R&D, engineering and design are essential inputs into product and process innovations, while telecommunications, and computer and information services, underpin the seamless transfer of knowledge and information that are the raw material of innovation, within and across borders. Finally, a host of business services help manufacturers relate to customers, suppliers and regulators. Also, mature industries are reinventing their business strategies in ways that rely more heavily on services as inputs. For example, consumer products such as clothing have shorter and more numerous seasons where market monitoring and market analysis feed back into design and production in order to keep up with consumers' ever shifting tastes.

Manufacturing firms increasingly add services to their product portfolio, typically as complements to the goods that they produce. Examples from the business-to-business market are machinery manufacturers that sell a services package to clients including the rental and maintenance of machinery. The machines are fitted with sensors linked back to suppliers through the IoT. Suppliers monitor performance continuously and help reduce maintenance costs and downtime for the client. Such arrangements are found for a broad range of machinery, from aircraft jet engines ("power by the hour") to copy machines or coffee machines in offices.

In the business-to-consumer market, after-sales services are major sources of revenue for manufacturers. The automotive sector, for instance, has relied on services for their revenues and profits for many years.[6] Today, with growing traffic congestion and environmental concerns, self-driving cars and various car-sharing and car-hailing services have shifted the focus from the car to the transport services it provides. All the major automotive manufacturers have teamed up with car-hailing services, car rental or leasing services or software and geo-positioning services, bringing joint provision of manufactured goods and services to a new level. Finally, visibility on social media has become indispensable in consumer markets and in many cases comes with innovative ways of bundling goods and services. In the food industry, for example, recipes and nutrition advice on social media play a prominent role in positioning products. In general, consumer products are increasingly marketed on social media as elements of the lifestyle of the targeted market segment.

The joint supply of goods and services is sometimes a defensive response to tougher competition rather than a creative process designing premium products. Moreover, it has costs and, for some manufacturers, smaller profit margins and a higher risk of bankruptcy. A number of case studies demonstrate that successful joint supply relies on well-integrated services, product and information modules, using IT systems that standardise and modularise the bundled services.[7]

Knowledge-capturing products: Making services tradable across-borders

The services sector is constantly evolving, adding new services and rendering others obsolete through a combination of deeper division of labour and technology. To capture the dynamics of the services sectors, the most recent manual for national accounts (SNA, 2008) added a separate category labelled knowledge-capturing products, defined as follows:

"Knowledge-capturing products concern the provision, storage, communication and dissemination of information, advice and entertainment in such a way that the consuming unit can access the knowledge repeatedly." [SNA, 2008, paragraph 6.22][8]

This category differs from other services in two important ways: the product can be stored and it can be accessed and used repeatedly. These are also the properties that make services tradable across borders without direct interaction between services supplier and customer.[9] Furthermore, repeated use at near-zero additional cost makes huge productivity gains possible.

New policy challenges emerge with the proliferation of knowledge-capturing products. Near-zero marginal costs are associated with very significant economies of scale that may result in "winner takes all" dynamics. Moreover, in a borderless digital economy the winners may be global while regulators operate within national borders. Another policy challenge related to repeated use at near-zero cost concerns the currently established systems for enforcing intellectual property and associated commercial rights, privacy and security. As knowledge and information go digital, the functionality of these systems needs to be assessed.

In sum, a rising share of services in the global economy has been observed for decades, and reflects both demand and technology factors. As people become richer, older and more urban they consume relatively more services. Many services sectors are catching up with manufacturing as far as productivity is concerned. Finally, goods and services are closely related and need to be understood as complementary inputs in production and consumption.

Trade in services

The great trade slowdown: Services as an engine of global trade growth

The value of global trade has stagnated since the financial crisis began in 2008. In the decade before the crisis, world trade grew almost twice as fast as world GDP, but in recent post-crisis years, world trade has lagged behind world GDP growth. Figure 1.3 compares trade in goods and services since 2005, three years before the crisis. Merchandise and

Figure 1.3. **World exports since the financial crisis**
Value index, 2008 = 100

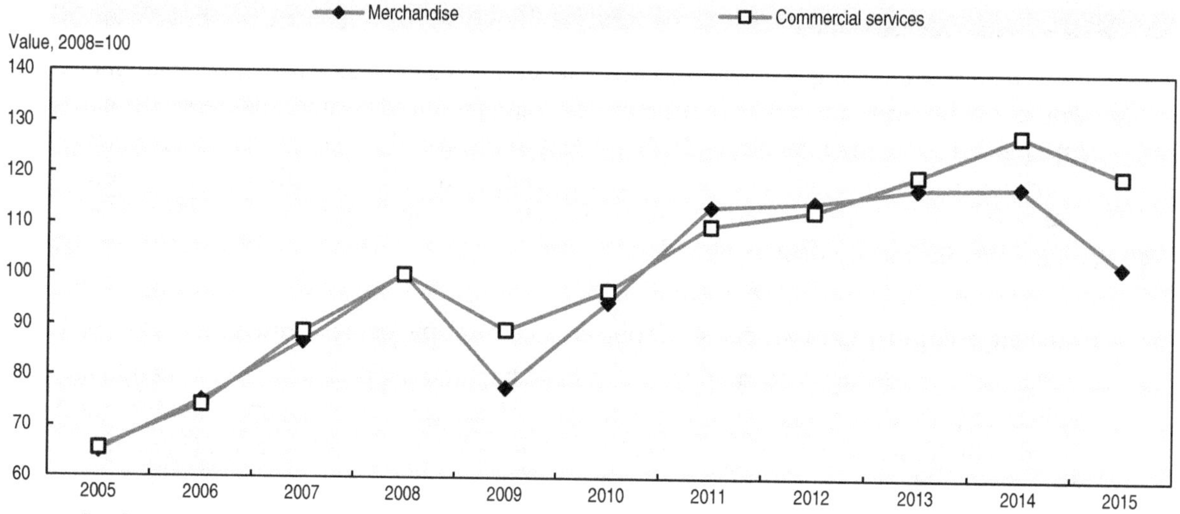

Source: Authors' estimates based on WTO statistics.

commercial services exports follow a similar pattern, but services exports are significantly less volatile than merchandise trade. Possible explanations for more resilient services trade are that demand is less cyclical, services are less dependent on external finance and they faced fewer protectionist measures after the crisis (Borchert and Mattoo, 2010). However, when measured in value-added terms, services trade is not more resilient than goods trade. Bearing in mind the high share of traded services that is embodied in other sectors' exports (see below), this is not surprising (Nagengast and Stehrer, 2016).

The great trade slowdown can only partly be explained by depressed demand in the global economy during the crisis and the shallow recovery. Structural changes, notably the levelling off and in some cases the unwinding of global value chains, also seem to be important causal factors, which means that trade cannot be expected to grow faster than the world economy in the foreseeable future (Haugh et al., 2016). Gains from fragmentation of production stem from deepening specialisation, economies of scale in production of each component and exploiting comparative advantage at the task level. However, fragmentation also has costs. Longer supply chains imply higher risk of disruption should one link in the chain falter, and transaction costs and co-ordination costs increase with the level of complexity. Some supply chains have matured and reached the point where the cost of further fragmentation outweighs the benefits. China has been a key player in global value chains and a source of trade in intermediate inputs. Over time, China has increased domestic value-added both through rising local capacity and foreign direct investment, and its imports of parts and components relative to total exports have steadily declined since the mid-1990s. Therefore, until new drivers of trade appear, it is probable that world trade will continue to track the pace of global GDP growth. In this light, trade in services, particularly digitally-delivered cross-border trade, holds the promise of becoming a new engine of international trade. If large economies like India were to embrace globalisation, this would also contribute significantly to world trade and growth.

Trade in goods and services complement each other

Services have always been traded. Indeed, international transport is as old as trade itself, and finance and insurance followed shortly after. Even today, transport and travel account for about half of world trade in commercial services, down from about 70% in 1980. The most dynamic part of services trade is business services, broadly defined to include telecommunications, computer and information services, finance and a host of other business services, including KIBS. The composition of world commercial services trade by broad categories is depicted in Figure 1.4. The United States is by far the largest exporter and also the largest importer, closely followed by China on the import side. Transport and travel dominate in most countries on both the export and import side. It is noted that China runs a significant deficit in transport and travel services, mirroring the shipment of its manufactured exports.

A high degree of specialisation in business services is observed in Ireland (where communications services are the largest exports), Luxembourg (where financial services make up the bulk of exports), and India, the United Kingdom, Switzerland and the Netherlands (which all export a broad range of business services). India ranks first in exports of communications services, largely driven by computer services, while the United States is the leading exporter of other business services. With 68%, India has the largest share of business services in commercial services exports, followed by Brazil with 58%. The composition of imports is similar to that of exports, although business services are much

Figure 1.4. **Commercial services trade by country, 2015**

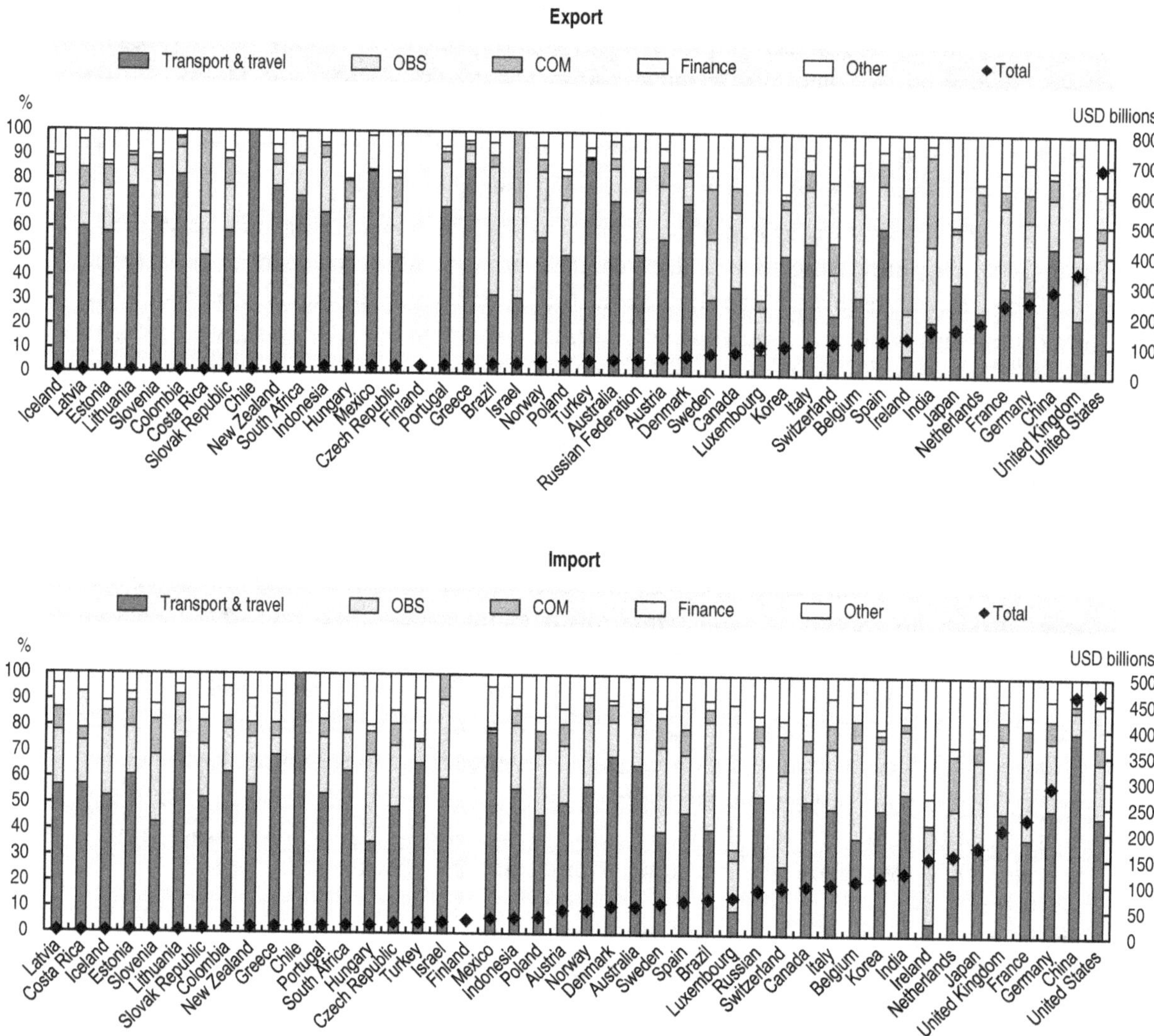

Note: COM = communications, including telecommunications, computer and information services. OBS = professional services, R&D services, management services and a number of technical services. Finance includes insurance. Other denotes all other commercial services. Data for Chile is for 2014. Data for Finland is reported only for aggregate total services.

The statistical data for Israel are supplied by and under the responsibility of the relevant Israeli authorities. The use of such data by the OECD is without prejudice to the status of the Golan Heights, East Jerusalem and Israeli settlements in the West Bank under the terms of international law.

Source: WTO; BPM6 classification.

more important in Japan's imports than its exports. It is notable that the most specialised countries, Ireland and Luxembourg, also import more business services than average. Luxembourg engages in extensive intra-industry trade in financial services, while Ireland's services trade patterns reflect its role as a hub for foreign investment in technology sectors. The largest exports are communications services while the largest imports are charges for the use of intellectual property. The United States and India demonstrate a substantial services trade surplus, while China accounts for the largest services trade deficit.

Figure 1.5 reports total growth in exports of communications and other business services compared to overall services exports over the decade to 2015. With the exceptions of Turkey and Indonesia, other business services and communications services gained ground in all countries depicted. China, closely followed by India, saw the fastest growth in services exports over the past decade, while Italy and South Africa lagged somewhat behind. Eight countries more than doubled their services exports during this period (from Costa Rica and rightwards in Figure 1.5). Korea, followed by China, Poland and Costa Rica experienced a very rapid growth in communications services exports, while Luxembourg and Costa Rica exhibit the fastest export growth in other business services. In contrast, Indonesia displays both a low level and slow growth in business services exports.

Figure 1.5. **Export value, 2005-15 by country**

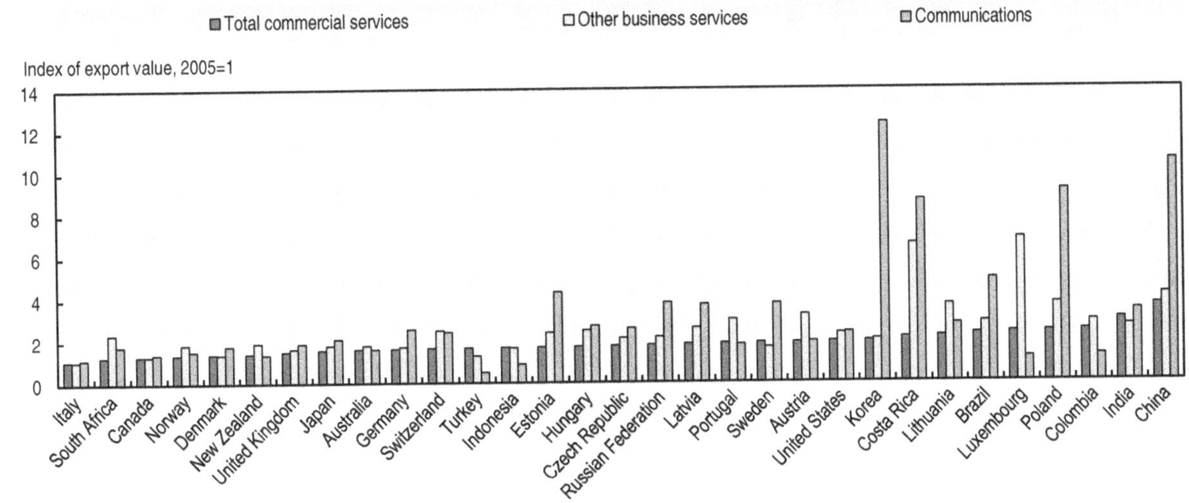

Note: "Communication" covers telecommunications, computer services and information services. "Other business services" aggregates professional services, R&D services, management services and a number of technical services.
Source: WTO; BPM6 classification.

The composition of services trade has changed over the past few decades, as business services have become more prominent. Even so, goods and services trade flows still move in lockstep with each other. Services accounted for 22% of world trade in 2015 and have hovered around 20% for the entire period for which data exist. Furthermore, this pattern also holds for individual countries as illustrated in Figure 1.8, which plots services trade against goods trade from 1960 to the present. Only a few observations fall outside the big cloud of highly correlated goods and services trades.[10] Thus, goods and services trade are still two sides of the same coin. As manufacturing production networks become more complex, supporting services become more complex too.

In addition to what can be gleaned from analysing aggregate trade data, an in-depth analysis of global value chains shows that about three quarters of trade in services consists of intermediate inputs for the production of goods and services (De Backer and Miroudot, 2013). This is a much higher share than for intermediate goods, which stands at about half. The important role of services in supporting other sectors' exports is also reflected in the ratio of value-added to gross exports. For manufacturing, this ratio declined from about 0.65 to 0.45 from 1970 to 2010. By contrast, for services, the same ratio increased from about 1.3 to 1.6 over the same period. A fall in this ratio signifies that intermediate inputs from other sectors and from abroad account for a rising share of the gross export value. A ratio above one as observed for services seems counterintuitive. However, when measured in value-added terms, services embodied in exports of other sectors contribute to the

Figure 1.6. **Trade in goods and services: Two sides of the same coin**

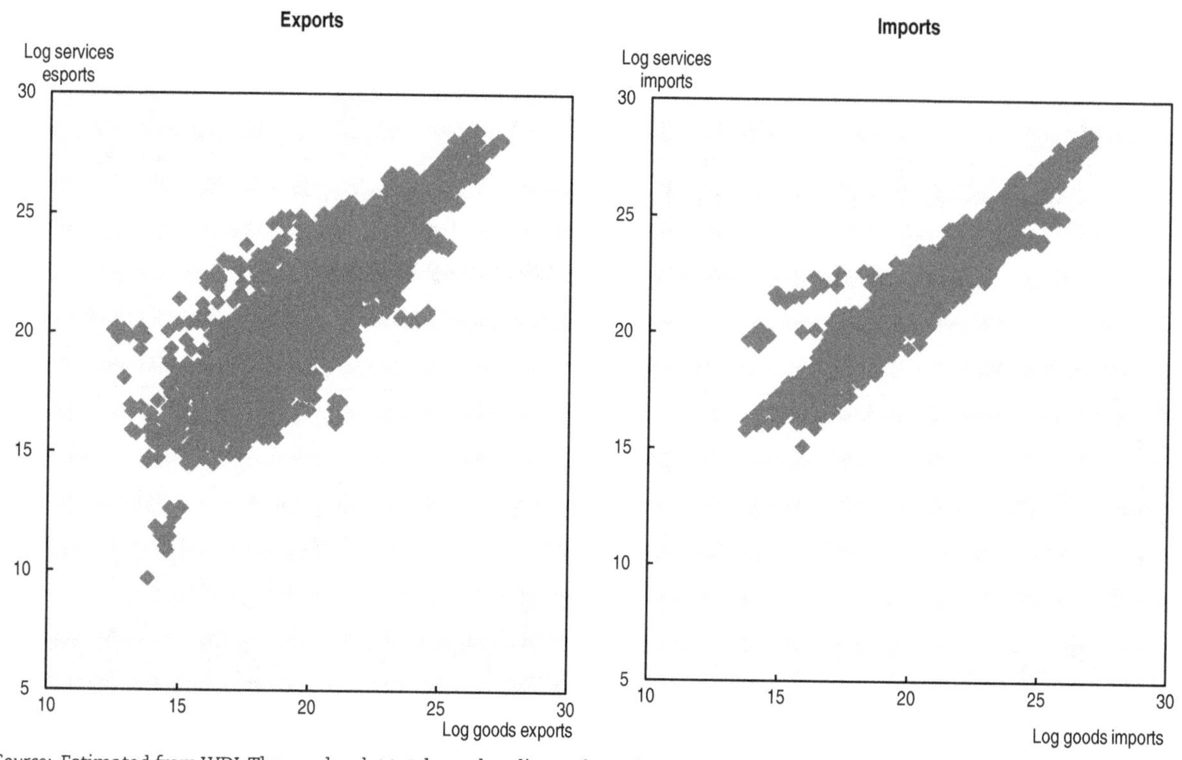

Source: Estimated from WDI. The graphs plot total merchandise trade against total commercial services trade for all countries in the WDI for the period 1960 to 2015.

numerator, while gross exports of services include services exported directly only. A ratio above one then means that more services are exported indirectly embodied in goods than are directly exported (Johnson and Noguera, 2016).

Externally-sourced services are important inputs in the fabrication and marketing of goods, but goods-producing firms also provide a range of services in-house and some of these are exported. Indeed across the countries included in the OECD/WTO Trade in Value Added (TiVA) database between 25% and 60% of employment in manufacturing firms is in services support functions (Miroudot and Cadestin, 2017). For example, multinational manufacturing firms often accompany affiliate production of goods abroad with headquarter services related to the design, production process management and quality control of their products. Manufacturers also combine shipment of goods with installation, maintenance and customer services. As illustrated in Figure 1.7, exports of architecture and engineering from manufacturing firms outpace those of specialised professional services firms in Belgium, Germany and Italy.[11] In-depth analysis of Belgian export patterns at the firm level shows that firms that export both goods and services account for about 30% of services exporters and realise 36% of services exports sales in the sectors covered by the analysis.

Cross-border services trade is highly concentrated in three dimensions: Firms, markets and products

The digital economy has in principle opened new opportunities for services firms, including SMEs, to engage in international trade. Nevertheless, entering and staying in export markets is not for the faint-hearted. The absolute number of successful micro- and small enterprises that are "born global" (Box 1.2) is sufficiently large to inspire and to

Figure 1.7. Distribution of exports between services and non-services firms, by sector

Selected services and countries

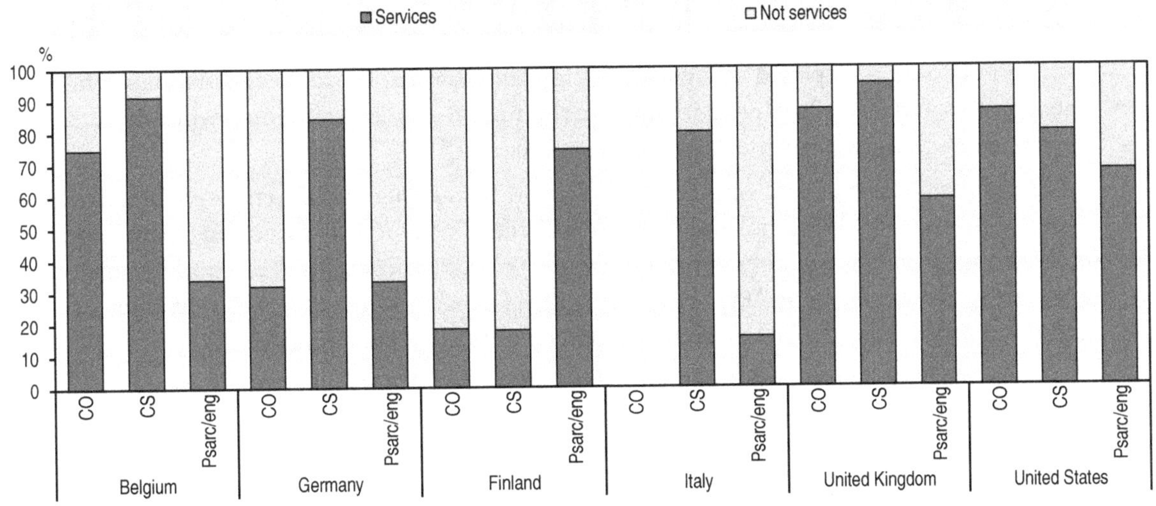

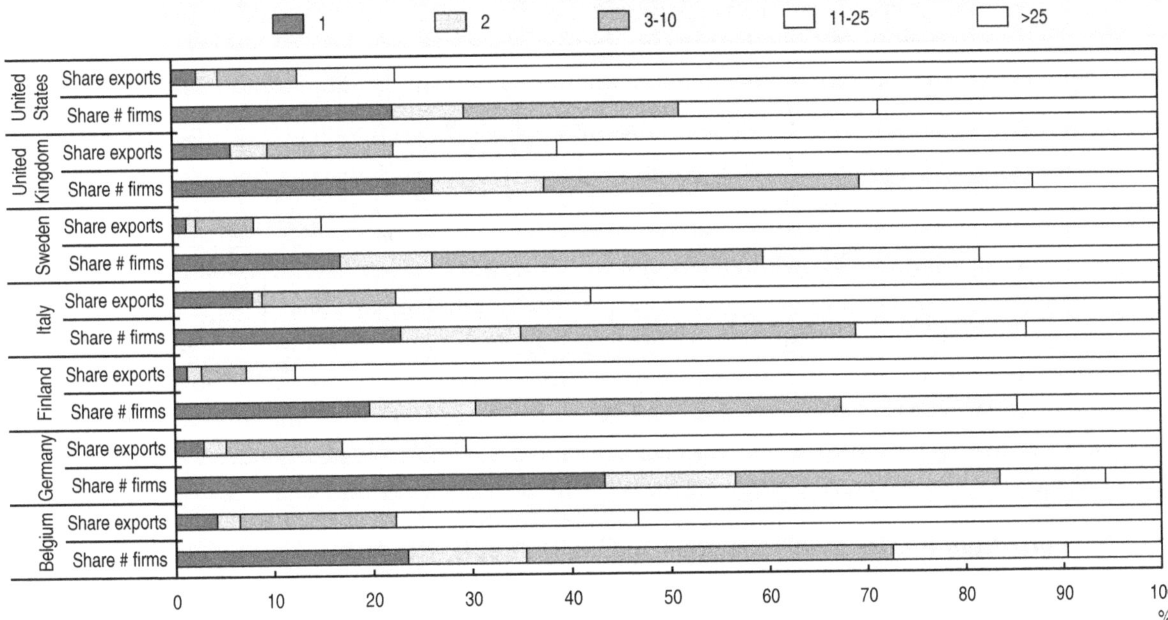

Note: CO = construction services, CS = computer services and PSarc/eng = architecture and engineering.
Source: Rouzet et al. (2017).

instigate various policy initiatives to encourage others to follow suit. Nevertheless, exporters are generally significantly larger and more productive than non-exporters, and more likely to be foreign-owned. Furthermore, most firms that export do so to only one foreign market, usually a neighbouring country or a country with which the home country has a free-trade agreement covering services.[12]

Figure 1.8 illustrates the high rate of concentration of exports once a firm has entered foreign markets. The share of exporting firms that export to only one foreign market ranges between 17% in Sweden and 43% in Germany, but their share of total export value

Figure 1.8. Concentration of international activity by number of destinations

Source: Rouzet et al. (2017).

is very small, amounting to between 1% and 6%. Conversely, the share of exporting firms that export to more than 25 destinations is only between 6% and 29%, but these exporters' share of total exports ranges from 53% (Belgium) and 88% (Finland). However, even the big exporters are highly dependent on their top destination market. For example, in the sample of countries depicted in Figure 1.8, the firms that export to 20 destinations send between 40% and 80% of their export value to their number one destination, which in turn absorbs more than twice as much as the second market.[13]

A similar pattern of concentration is found for the number of different services a firm exports. Between 36% (Finland) and 70% (United States) of exporting firms export only one product, accounting for between 2% (Finland) and 37% (Belgium) of total exports. Conversely, between 4% and 18% of exporting firms export five or more different services, and these account for the largest share of total exports (Rouzet et al., 2017).

Evidence from Germany shows that between 20% and 40% of all cross-border services exporters only export occasionally. The incidence of one-time exporters is highest in the construction sector and lowest for courier services. About two-fifths of all export relationships are terminated after one year in construction and about one-fifth in courier services. Courier services are also the sector exhibiting the longest duration of trade spells with two-fifths of all export relationships lasting for ten years or more. The sector has been boosted by cross-border e-commerce and just-in-time production networks that traverse international borders. By contrast, in the construction services sector only about a tenth of export relationships last for ten consecutive years or more. A relatively short duration of export relationships is also found in architecture and engineering services. A possible explanation is that exports of services related to the construction and building industry may be project-based and terminate with the completion of the project.

The firm-level evidence suggests that entering a foreign market is hard and costly, and costs increase more than proportionally with the number of destinations and products a firm sells abroad. When entering a new market, potential exporters might "test the waters" to assess the local conditions before deciding whether to invest in durable buyer-supplier relationships. In many cases, such experimentation fails and new entrants exit quickly. Only the most productive and innovative among first-time exporters manage to establish a foothold in the market and thereafter strengthen their presence and increase export sales.

Services that cannot be stored and consumed repeatedly are traded through face-to-face interaction between suppliers and customers, or they travel with the products that are transformed by the services, e.g. in transport. To bring such services under the realm of international trade agreements, the definition of services trade has been extended from cross-border trade to cover trade through consumption abroad, commercial presence abroad, and cross-border movement of people. The relative importance of these different modes of supply is not well understood, but a pilot study by Eurostat (2016) on extra-EU trade found that foreign affiliate sales (Mode 3) account for 69% of services trade, cross-border trade (Mode 1) 21%, consumption abroad (Mode 2) 6% and services supplied by natural persons (Mode 4) 4% in 2013.[14] Brazil's services exports exhibit a similar pattern.[15] Clearly, trade through commercial presence dwarfs the other modes of supply.

Foreign affiliate sales dwarf the other modes of supply, but follow similar patterns to cross-border trade

Information on global foreign affiliate sales is not available, but data on the stock of FDI by sector exists for a number of OECD countries. It is not a perfect proxy for affiliate sales but nevertheless sheds light on the relative importance of services in multinational activities. Figure 1.9 shows that the services share of multinational enterprise activity is in line with the services share of GDP and employment. A closer look at the composition of services FDI assets by sector across 24 OECD countries reveals that financial services play a dominant role, on average accounting for more than half the stock of FDI held abroad and more than 40% of the stock of FDI from abroad.

Figure 1.9. **Foreign direct investment stock, 2015**

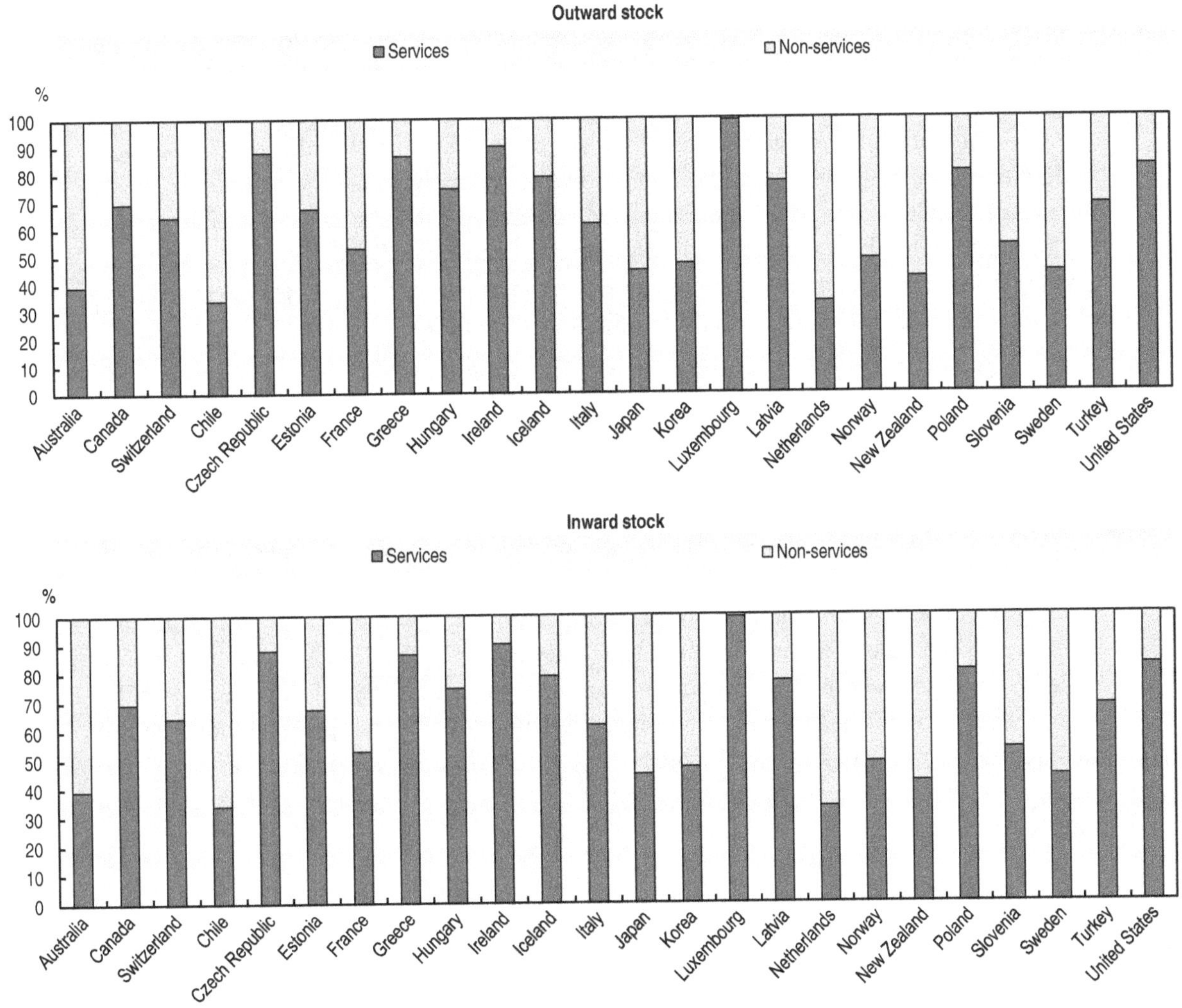

Outward stock

■ Services ☐ Non-services

Inward stock

■ Services ☐ Non-services

Source: OECD FDI statistics.

A study of affiliate sales at the firm level in selected countries reveals similar patterns as for cross-border trade. The countries included in the analyses are Finland, Germany, Italy, Japan, the United Kingdom, and the United States.[16] Multinational services firms tend to be larger and more productive than local firms, including local firms that engage in cross-border exports. Foreign affiliate sales per product and export destination are on average more than ten times larger than cross-border exports.

Multinational services providers are few and far between relative to the number of cross-border services exporters. Yet their foreign affiliate sales account for the bulk of total services trade through all modes. In Germany, foreign affiliate sales account for as much as 80% of total services exports in most sectors. Like services exporters, multinational firms tend to depend heavily on their largest host market, which is typically a market close to home. European multinationals, for example, tend to establish mainly in other EU countries, although the United States is the most important host for UK multinationals measured by the number of affiliate firms. Conversely, the United Kingdom is the most important host market for US services multinationals measured by affiliate sales. China figures prominently as a host for German and Japanese multinationals, taking second place among the top destinations for both. A surprisingly small share of cross-border services exports are undertaken by multinational services firms to the same country and in the same sector, suggesting that multimodal services trade is not very common, with the exception of maritime and air transport.

The characteristic for which there are significant qualitative differences between multinational services firms and cross-border traders is the composition by product type of their trade activity. Some of the most digitised sectors, computer services, architecture and engineering tend to be traded through cross-border exports, while distribution services are largely traded through commercial presence. For the other services sectors there is a large variation across countries in which mode of supply dominates.

To summarise, services exporters are larger and more productive than non-exporters and multinational services exporters are larger still. Foreign affiliate sales are by a wide margin the most important mode of supply, followed by cross-border trade. Services exporters, whether engaging in cross-border trade or affiliate sales, tend to concentrate their exports in one or a few destination markets and a few products. With widespread migration of services activities to the digital economy, one would expect cross-border supply to have grown faster and brought more SMEs into international markets than actually happened. As we shall see in following chapters, regulatory barriers to trade and investment affect SMEs disproportionately. Furthermore, in the KIBS sectors cross-border trade for value services are highly complementary to deploying staff at the premises of the clients for short periods. Chapter 2 demonstrates that movement of people tends to be the most restricted mode of supply, which could stifle cross-border trade significantly. A more recent concern for services traders is limitations on the flow of data needed to embark on a digital transformation.[17]

Services in the digital economy

Will professional services be automated?

The rise of services in international markets is to a large extent driven by the ICT revolution (Box 1.1). Once the output of a service activity can be codified, it can in principle also be digitised and transmitted over electronic networks globally. Professional services are a case in point. They generate knowledge-capturing products that can be stored and thereafter consumed and accessed repeatedly. Examples are professional services automation (PSA) software, which is gaining prominence in architecture, accounting, legal services and management consulting. Computer-assisted design that feeds into computer-assisted manufacturing forming CAD/CAM systems has been commonly used in a host of manufacturing industries for decades. What is new in more recent years is that CAD can be separated from CAM in time, space and institutionally.

Box 1.1. **Telecommunications and the digital economy**

Telecommunications form the backbone and infrastructure on which the digital economy is founded. According to Cisco, a leading network company, global internet traffic has grown from 100 gigabytes per day in 1992 to more than 20 000 gigabytes per second in 2015. The devices used for internet traffic are changing rapidly. While computers used to dominate, machine-to-machine (M2M) devices are currently the fastest growing devices, followed by smartphones and connected TVs. Nevertheless, PCs still account for the largest traffic share (67% in 2015), followed by smartphones and connected TVs. M2M connections are rapidly gaining ground in both consumer and business markets. The most prominent uses in the consumer markets are connected home applications and connected healthcare, while the fastest growing business services are a host of location-based services such as supply chain and fleet management and not least video conferencing. Growth in demand for more sophisticated digital products, such as video, and secure and reliable payment services and design, to mention but a few, clearly depend on high-speed and high quality connections. As of 2015, consumer traffic accounts for more than 80% of internet and managed IP traffic. Figure 1.10 depicts the broadband, mobile and Wi-Fi average speed by region in 2015.

There are large regional differences, with Asia Pacific-led by Korea and Japan-having the highest average broadband speed and North America the highest mobile and Wi-Fi speed. Latin America, Middle East and Africa lag relatively far behind, although they are forecasted to experience faster improvement during the next three years. It should also be borne in mind that the lagging regions not only have slower connections, they also have far fewer connections. Key to higher speed is investment in infrastructure, which in turn is facilitated by an open and well-regulated telecommunications sector (Nordås and Rouzet, 2016).

Figure 1.10. **Internet speed, 2015**

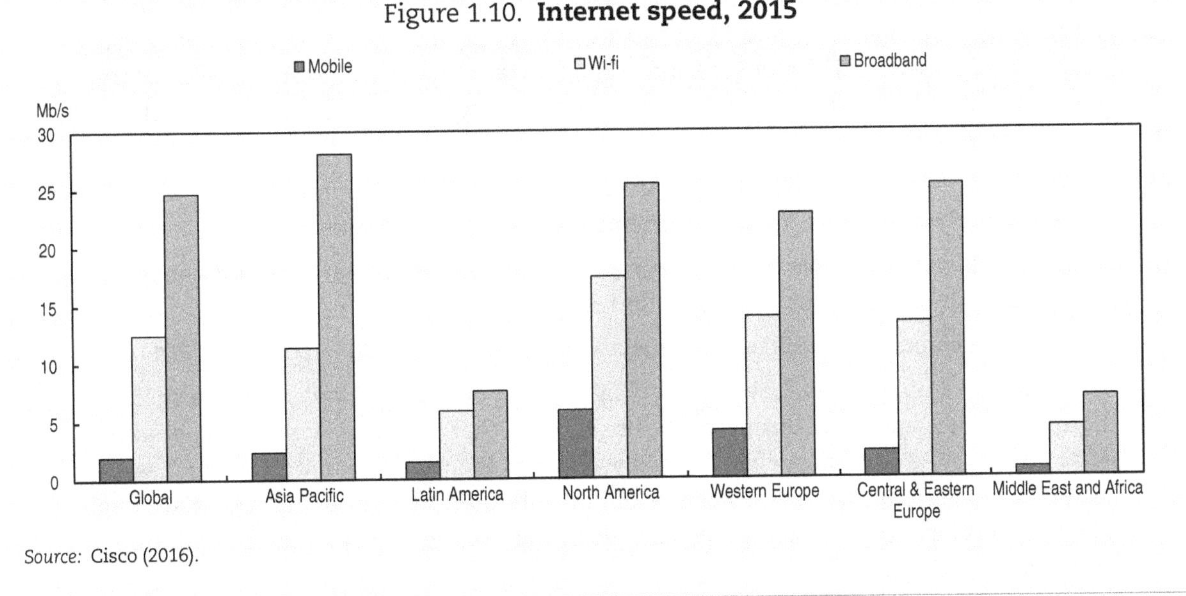

Source: Cisco (2016).

Knowledge can be digitised, but still needs to be explained

In business-to-business transactions, PSAs are mainly used as a tool by professionals to streamline their services and draw on accumulated experience from earlier projects. The core of their activities is, however, still the personal interaction with clients. Typical situations where firms need professional support are during the course of product and process innovation, when adopting a new technology, preparing for entering a new market or complying with new regulations. Facing changing market conditions, the managers and staff of, for example, manufacturing firms may lack the capacity to identify the opportunities available to them and the means to reap the benefits on their own even when they have access to online information. The typical business model of professional and other knowledge-intensive business services is therefore a combination of automated basic services provided over digital platforms and collaboration with clients to help find solutions when clients face important strategic decisions. The codified and tacit elements of KIBS activities are highly complementary and usually bundled under a contract with the client.

This does not mean that KIBS are not being disrupted by the digital revolution. Routine tasks such as filing tax returns, accounting, and a host of human resource management and customer management functions are increasingly performed through the use of PSAs. These can be bought off the shelf or as cloud-based software-as-a-service. In addition, modularisation is chipping away into the core of business services. Digitisation of professional services can be understood as a learning process. New, cutting-edge knowledge tends to be tacit, but over time it becomes better understood and once fully understood can be codified and digitised. Machine learning speeds up this process by identifying underlying commonalities and patterns in the information professionals and their clients amass.

Digitisation makes basic professional services affordable to consumers and SMEs

There are different views on how deeply digitisation will impact on professional services. All agree that routine services such as accounting and tax filing are moving online and individuals as well as SMEs may use solely online platforms for these purposes. The most radical view is that the exclusive right to provide certain services by licensed professionals is under attack as consumers and businesses can perform these services themselves using digital platforms. Susskind and Susskind (2015) provide a number of examples of platforms becoming the dominant channel for accessing knowledge traditionally provided by professionals, including:

- More disagreements between eBay traders are resolved through online dispute resolution each year than there are lawsuits filed in the entire US court system.

- In 2014, 48 million people filed tax returns using online tax preparation software rather than a tax professional in the United States.

- An online community designed and built a house for GBP 50 000 in London in 2014.

These examples could, however, also signify that online KIBS lower the threshold for both consumers and small businesses to use services that they otherwise could not afford. If so, online KIBS expand the customer base rather than undermining the business for licensed professional services. In line with that interpretation, others find that although the KIBS business model is being transformed by digitisation, the operations of KIBS are by and large unperturbed.[18]

The fact that it takes considerable skills and capacity on the user side to take full advantage of online business services may mitigate the impact of online services on traditional knowledge-intensive business services. In particular, the user must be able to formulate a problem in a concise manner and operationalise suggested solutions, which are important parts of the services package that KIBS suppliers offer. It is well documented in the literature that the take-up of online services is much smaller in SMEs than larger companies (OECD, 2017).

As will be demonstrated in more depth in following chapters, the potential for knowledge sharing and technology diffusion through international trade in professional services is far from being fully captured. Rather, markets are fragmented due to geographical, institutional, cultural and regulatory differences, and not least due to exclusive rights for certain professionals to provide a service in a specific jurisdiction. In addition, many countries prohibit multidisciplinary work across professions. As the borders between different professions are blurring, it may be time to re-think the relevant, century-old professional regulatory regimes.

Box 1.2. "Born global": Medium, small and micro-enterprises (MSMEs) in the digital economy

The concept of "born global" was introduced already in the early 1990s. It refers most commonly to a firm that started foreign operations within three years of inception and that derives at least 25% of its turnover from outside the home market. Several studies have found that important driving forces for going global early are a small home market, scalability of the product or a niche strategy. ICT products fit this description well. There is little systematic information on the number and nature of firms born global, but three broad categories can be identified: online market places, digital product applications and production networks combining online and offline activities

Local Motors is an example of a production network, combining online and offline activities. It also illustrates the complementarity between goods and services in a modern economy. The company was established in the United States in 2007, and specialises in custom-made vehicles. According to its website, it is an international community of enthusiasts, designers, engineers, fabricators and experts. The company had about 200 employees in 2016 (up from 15 in 2010), and about 50 000 community members all over the world that collaborate on designs across a number of projects. Designs are developed into projects through online collaboration and the cars are built on demand in micro-factories. The company owns micro-factories in the United States and one in Germany. The flagship project so far is a self-driving electrical vehicle named Olli (photo), while the most recent project is the first 3D printed electrical vehicle in the world (*https://localmotors.com/*).

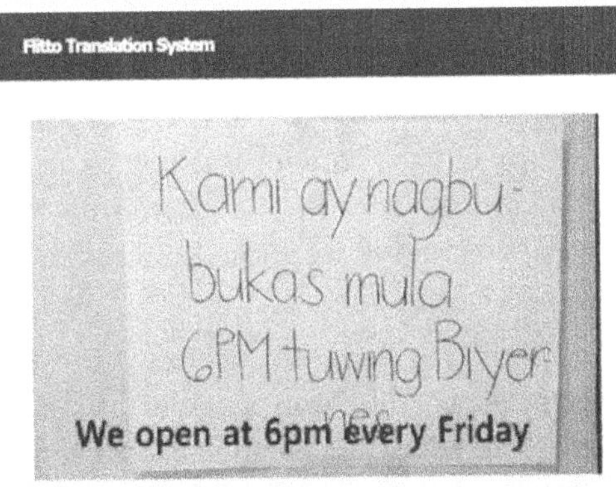

Flitto is an online market place as well as digital product application. Its business model is crowd-sourcing of translation services. The company was established in 2012 by three young Korean entrepreneurs who were selected for the SpringBoard incubator program in London. The Flitto app connects human translators with customers in real time and currently has six million users. Payment is based on points that can be bought or earned by providing translations. The app currently supports 17 languages, including Arabic, Chinese, English, French, German, Indonesian, Hindi, Japanese, Korean and Russian. Users can for instance take a photo of a hand-written note

---

> ### Box 1.2. **"Born global": Medium, small and micro-enterprises (MSMEs)**
> ### **in the digital economy** *(cont.)*
>
> with their smartphone, upload it to the Flitto app, and in a few minutes a translator will have translated it into the desired language as shown in the picture. Flitto also offers a one-to-one professional translation service. The main office is in Seoul employing about 40 people and the company has a branch office in Beijing. Revenue derives from a fee on transactions made on its app and the company also sells its database of translations to internet firms that use them for machine learning.
>
> *Source:* Flitto website *(www.flitto.com)* and presentation by Simon Lee, the CEO of Flitto, at an OECD/APEC workshop, 28 August 2015 .

The on-demand economy and platforms

Platforms are flourishing in labour-intensive services sectors such as transport, distribution, logistics, courier services, handyman services and a host of personal services. Indeed, there are platforms for almost any service. There is no unified definition, but most agree that a platform is essentially a piece of software, an operating system or a database on which other smaller application programs can be designed to run. Platforms provide a low-threshold market entry opportunity for entrepreneurs, hobbyists and SMEs, they reduce transaction costs substantially by gathering large amounts of data that support reputation and trust building, and they usually integrate secure payment systems.

Platforms and applications often rely significantly on innovation by users. For example, users have played a very important role in the development and diffusion of financial services provided over mobile networks and applications. Furthermore, such services first took hold in developing counties and have spread from there to developed countries. This is an example of need being the mother of invention as unbanked people in developing countries got access to mobile telephones (van der Boor et al., 2014). Mobile banking is but one so-called "fin-tech" product. Others that have emerged mostly in developed countries are peer-to-peer lending platforms, electronic exchanges and even robo-advisors, which do market analytics for investors.

The actual and potential contribution of platforms in service sectors to the overall economy has been debated in the literature. Is their main role to improve capacity utilisation by putting to work idle capital such as homes and cars, and to provide flexible work opportunities for those that would otherwise not work? For example, Airbnb, which is a market place for hospitality services founded in 2008, grew very rapidly and has currently more than 2 million listings, more than any hotel chain (Luca, 2017). Or are they opening new opportunities for individual services suppliers to compete with companies and for start-ups to go global from their inception? The quick answer is that platforms can be both a boon for consumers and entrepreneurs as the examples from the KIBS sectors and Box 1.2 demonstrate, while disrupting traditional service suppliers.

The labour market impact of platforms is one of the great social concerns in the global digital economy. It is clear that the relative importance of non-standard work has increased in recent years in most OECD countries (OECD, 2016), although it is less clear how this relates to digital platforms and globalisation of services. Non-standard work is defined as self-employed (own-account), temporary full-time employees and part-time employees. Among these, self-employed are probably the most relevant for platforms.[19]

As indicated in Figure 1.11, the share of self-employment in total civilian employment ranged between about 6% in Luxembourg and the United States and 51% in Colombia in 2015. Other countries with more than 30% of the labour force in self-employment are Greece (35%), Turkey (33%) and Mexico (32%). Of the 34 mainly OECD countries included in the data, only six (the Czech Republic, Estonia, Finland, the Netherlands, the Slovak Republic and the United Kingdom) saw a rise in self-employment during the period 2000-15. Among these, the largest increase was observed in the Slovak Republic, the Netherlands and the United Kingdom. In the other 28 countries, the self-employment rate declined between 2000 and 2015.

Figure 1.11. **Self-employment percentage of civilian labour force**

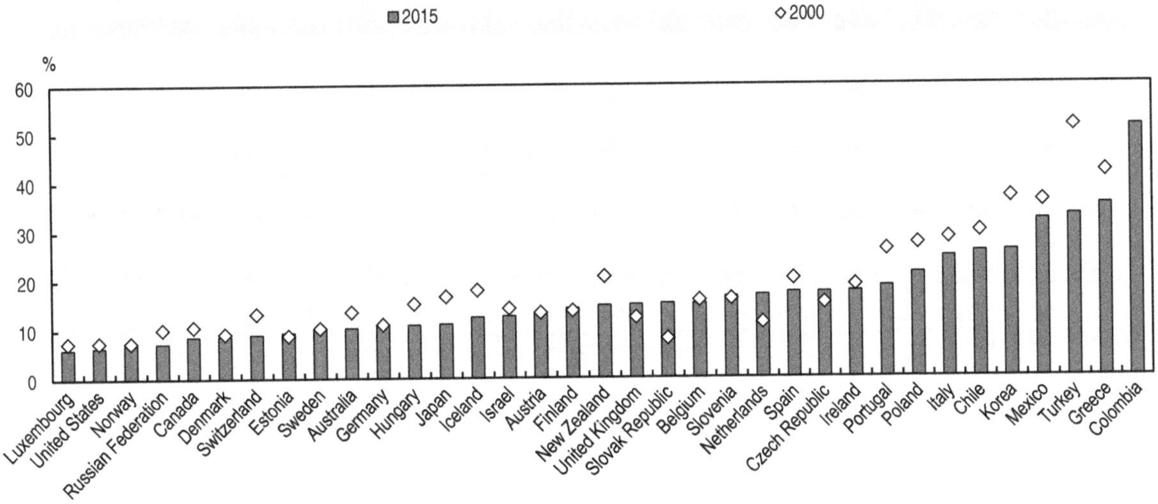

Source: OECD.stat.

Self-employment includes many more activities than those facilitated by platforms, and as of yet, platforms seem to play a marginal role. Thus, recent estimates from the United States suggest that the share of the labour force working with labour platforms is between 0.4% and 0.9%. Labour services provided over platforms continue to grow rapidly, but not as fast as in the recent past (Farrell and Greig, 2016; Katz and Krueger, 2016).[20] A common finding is that there is a high rate of churning in these activities. Less than half of the participants on the supply side stay with the platform for more than 12 months and about a sixth of participants in any month are newcomers. Finally, average monthly earnings on labour platforms declined between 2014 and 2016 (Farrell and Greig, 2016).

Platforms: Natural monopolies?

Platforms not only connect suppliers and customers, they are also businesses in their own right. The best-known digital platforms are relatively young and they have grown very rapidly to dominate the industry in which they operate. The strategic asset of platforms is information extracted from the participants. The more participants, the more information is gathered and the more valuable the platform is, creating a positive feed-back loop. More participants on one side of the multi-sided platforms attract more participants on the other side, inducing rapid growth after a critical mass is obtained. Conversely, if a platform fails to attract a critical mass within the first few years, it quickly disappears. Successful platforms can therefore dominate markets completely, and in some cases they exhibit characteristics of natural monopolies. They are typically global in scope and, depending on the market they operate in, they may connect suppliers and customers in a local market (e.g. for personal services) or in a global market (e.g. film, music, design, software-as-a-service).

The implications of dominant global platforms for competition policy are subject to debate. The commonly used tools for identifying significant market power, such as market share, pricing above average long-run costs or profit margins do not apply to multisided markets (e.g. Evans and Schmalensee, 2013; Evans, 2016). More rigorous methodology that takes into account all sides of the market on a case-by-case basis is needed to determine whether or not anti-trust remedies are needed.

To summarise this section, digitisation lies at the heart of both productivity gains in services and making services tradable across borders. Like technological revolutions in the past, digitisation brings huge potential gains to consumers and disrupts existing markets, business models and not least the labour market.

Concluding remarks

A rising share of services in employment and consumption is observed across the globe and is explained by a combination of technical progress, urbanisation and demand factors. Technology has reduced trade and transaction costs for both goods and services, thereby facilitating a deeper division of labour and more complex and services-intensive production networks. The close relationship between trade in goods and services is also underscored by the fact that a greater volume of exported services is embodied in products from other sectors than those exported directly. Moreover, three-quarters of services exported directly across borders are intermediate inputs suggesting that cross-border trade in services represent largely business-to-business (B2B) transactions. As a consequence, trade in goods and services follow each other in lockstep and should be seen as complementary activities in international markets. It follows that policy measures restricting trade in services impede trade in both services and goods.

Cross-border services trade accounts for only about 20% of total cross-border trade, and has remained fairly constant for decades. With the digital transformation of services one would expect a rising share of services traded directly to consumers through platforms, applications and other forms of electronic networks. So far, it appears that a global digital services economy remains elusive. There are many reasons for this. First, tradable tasks and modules are complementary to less tradable components. For example, knowledge can be codified, digitised and traded, but needs to be interpreted and sometimes explained by a natural person at the receiving end. Second, entering foreign markets can be costly and most firms, particularly SMEs, choose to focus on their home market. Third, cross-border services trade is still impeded by a number of regulatory obstacles, particularly in cases where a license is required to provide services and when occasional face-to-face interaction between client and services suppliers is needed.

The services share of foreign investment stocks on the other hand is closer to the services share of GDP. This does not mean that services trade through foreign affiliate sales is open and free. Rather, it suggests that the drivers and impediments to foreign investment may be of a similar magnitude for goods and services. There are, however, quite significant variations across sectors. For example, financial services play an outsized role in services trade through affiliate sales. Financial services support all economic activities, including trade and international commerce, and are subject to stringent regulation or outright prohibition of cross-border trade. In addition, financial services providers must assess the risks associated with clients and markets, which may be easier with a commercial presence in each market. Both regulation and the preferred business model may thus tilt financial services trade towards mode 3. The policy determinants of trade in services are explored in detail in the next chapter.

Notes

1. Source: World Development Indicators (WDI). The time series for middle income countries go back to 1960 when the share of services in GDP stood at 36.5%. Rodrik (2016) found that, between 1970 and 2013, the manufacturing share of GDP measured at constant prices remained stable both globally and in the United States, rose significantly in China and in the rest of Asia, and declined somewhat everywhere else.

2. For a fascinating chronicle of how technology, trade and the rise of modern services have transformed the life of ordinary Americans, see Gordon (2016). See also De Backer et al. (2016) for an assessment of labour market impacts of reshoring.

3. The productivity measure presented here is total factor productivity (TFP), which tabulates the change in output volume relative to changes in the use of inputs including capital, labour and intermediate inputs. If output volume increases faster than the volume of inputs, then TFP increases. The EU_KLEMS database contains updated TFP figures for only ten countries of which the three largest and one small economy have been selected. Data from the United States show similar patterns, with manufacturing productivity growth falling behind many services categories during the same period. The sector classification is, however, different and information is available at different levels of aggregation.

4. In France and the United Kingdom, employment in retail and wholesale trade is higher than in manufacturing.

5. See, for instance, Aarikka-Stenroos and Jaakkola (2012), Amiti and Wei (2009), Ciriaci et al. (2015) and Rubalcaba and Kox (2007).

6. A recent note by Arthur D. Little reports that after-sales services accounted for 23% of revenue and 54% of profits in the car industry in 2015. *www.adlittle.com/downloads/tx_adlreports/AMG_Automotive_after_sales_2015_01.pdf*

7. In the business literature, this phenomenon is referred to as the servitisation paradox (Gebauer et al., 2005; Cenamour et al., 2016).

8. See *http://unstats.un.org/unsd/nationalaccount/sna.asp*.

9. Some authors have labelled knowledge-intensive activities "quaternary services", seeing them as comprising a qualitatively new sector splitting off from the tertiary sector.

10. The three observations below the cloud in the export chart represent Iceland in the 1960s. Iceland later developed strong services exports, particularly in air transport. The observations to the left of the cloud represent Tuvalu, whose exports are largely concentrated in the tourism sector.

11. Information on international activities by firms is not readily available. The statistical agencies of the countries included in the analysis kindly allowed us to analyse anonymised data under strict confidentiality conditions. The following disclaimers apply: This work contains statistical data from ONS which is Crown Copyright. The use of the ONS statistical data in this work does not imply the endorsement of the ONS in relation to the interpretation or analysis of the statistical data. This work uses research datasets which may not exactly reproduce National Statistics aggregates. The statistical analysis of firm-level US data on multinational companies and services exporters was conducted at the Bureau of Economic Analysis, US Department of Commerce under arrangements that maintain legal confidentiality requirements. The views expressed are those of the authors and do not reflect official positions of the Department of Commerce.

12. See, for instance, Wagner (2012) for a recent review of the descriptive literature on patterns of foreign trade analysing firm-level data.

13. The distribution of exports on destination markets appears to follow a Pareto distribution.

14. See Eurostat (2016) *http://ec.europa.eu/eurostat/statistics-explained/index.php?title=Services_trade_statistics_by_modes_of_supply&oldid=320612*.

15. See Rouzet et al. (2017), where commercial presence is estimated at 69% of total, cross-border trade 23% and consumption abroad 8%. Trade through movement of people contributes only marginally.

16. For an in-depth analysis, see Rouzet et al. (2017).

17. For a typology of such measures, along with a discussion of the use of data by business and possible impacts of measures, see Lopez-Gonzalez et al.

18. See World Economic Forum White Paper (2017).

19. There have been some disputes over the extent to which labour platforms such as Uber should be considered equivalent to employment. The criteria appear to be to what extent the platform controls the conduct, price, work hours, and work conditions of the participants. A recent court ruling in the United Kingdom, for example, found that Uber drivers must be considered employees. The ruling has been appealed. *www.judiciary.gov.uk/wp-content/uploads/2016/10/aslam-and-farrar-v-uber-reasons-20161028.pdf.*

20. Labour platforms are defined as platforms that connect customers with freelance or contingent workers who perform discrete tasks or projects. Growth in labour platform participation year-on-year was 102% in July 2016, down from almost 500% in July 2014.

References

Aarikka-Stenroos, L. and E. Jaakkola (2012), "Value co-creation in knowledge intensive business services: A dyadic perspective on the joint problem solving process", *Industrial Marketing Management*, Vol. 41, pp. 15-26.

Amiti, M. and S.-J. Wei (2009), "Services offshoring and productivity: Evidence from the US", *The World Economy*, Vol. 32, pp. 203-220.

Benz, S., A. Khanna and H.K. Nordås (2017), "Services and performance of the Indian economy: Analysis and policy options", *OECD Trade Policy Papers*, No. 196, OECD Publishing, Paris, *http://dx.doi.org/10.1787/9259fd54-en.*

Borchert, I. and A. Mattoo (2010), "The crisis resilience of services trade", *The Services Industry Journal*, Vol. 30, pp. 2115-2136.

Ciriaci, A., S. Montresor and D. Palma (2015), "Do KIBS make manufacturing more innovative? An empirical investigation of four European countries", *Technological Forecasting and Social Change*, Vol. 95, pp. 35-151.

Cisco (2016), "The zettabyte era: Trends and analysis", *www.cisco.com/c/en/us/solutions/collateral/service-provider/visual-networking-index-vni/vni-hyperconnectivity-wp.html.*

De Backer, K. and S. Miroudot (2013), "Mapping global value chains", *OECD Trade Policy Papers*, No. 159, OECD Publishing, Paris, *http://dx.doi.org/10.1787/5k3v1trgnbr4-en.*

De Backer, K., C. Menon, I. Desnoyers-James and L. Moussiegt (2016), "Reshoring: Myth or reality?", *OECD Science, Technology and Industry Policy Papers*, No. 27, OECD Publishing, Paris, *http://dx.doi.org/10.1787/5jm56frbm38s-en.*

Evans, D.S. (2016), "Multisided platforms, dynamic competition, and the assessment of market power for internet-based firms", *Chicago Coase-Sandor Institute for Law and Economics Working Paper*, No. 753, *https://papers.ssrn.com/sol3/papers.cfm?abstract_id=2746095.*

Evans, D.S. and R. Schmalensee (2013), "The antitrust analysis of multi-sided platforms businesses", *NBER Working Paper no 18783*, *www.nber.org/papers/w18783.pdf.*

Eurostat (2016), "Services trade statistics by mode of supply" Statistics Explained, *http://ec.europa.eu/eurostat/statistics-explained/index.php?title=Services_trade_statistics_by_modes_of_supply&oldid=310579.*

Farrell, D. and F. Greig (2016), "The online platform economy: Has growth peaked?", JP Morgan Chase &Co. Institute, November, *www.jpmorganchase.com/corporate/institute/document/jpmc-institute-online-platform-econ-brief.pdf.*

Gebauer, H., E. Fleisch and T. Friedli (2005), "Overcoming the services paradox in manufacturing companies", *European Management Journal*, Vol. 23, pp. 14-26.

Gordon, R.J. (2016), *The rise and fall of American growth: The US standard of living since the Civil War*, Princeton University Press, Princeton, New Jersey.

Haugh, D., A. Kopoin, E. Rusticelli, D. Turner and R. Dutu (2016), "Cardiac arrest or dizzy spell: Why is world trade so weak and what can policy do about it?", *OECD Economic Policy Papers*, No. 18, OECD Publishing, Paris, *http://dx.doi.org/10.1787/5jlr2h45q532-en*.

Johnson, R.C. and G. Noguera (2016), "A portrait of trade in value added over four decades", *NBER Working Paper 22974*, World Trade Organization, *www.wto.org/english/res_e/reser_e/ersd201702_e.pdf*.

Katz, L. and A. Krueger (2016), "The rise and nature of alternative work arrangements in the United States, 1995-2015", *NBER Working Paper no 22667*, September, *www.nber.org/papers/w22667*.

Lodefalk, M. and H.K. Nordås (2017), "Trading firms and trading costs in services: The case of Sweden", Örebro University, School of Business Working Paper (forthcoming).

Lopez-Gonzalez, J., D. Flaig, M.-A. Jouanjean, J. Messent, M. Rentzhog and P. Walkenhorst (forthcoming) "Localising data in a globalised world", *OECD Trade Policy Papers*, OECD Publishing, Paris.

Luca, M. (2017), "Designing online market places: Trust and reputation mechanisms", *Harvard Business School Working Paper*, No. 17-017, *www.hbs.edu/faculty/Publication%20Files/17-017_ec4ccdc0-4348-4eb9-9f46-86e1ac696b4f.pdf*.

Miroudot, S. and C. Cadestin (2017), "Services in global value chains: From inputs to value-creating activities", *OECD Trade Policy Papers*, No. 197, OECD Publishing, Paris, *http://dx.doi.org/10.1787/465f0d8b-en*.

Nagengast, A.J. and R. Stehrer (2016), "The great collapse in value added trade", *Review of International Economics*, Vol. 24, pp. 392-421.

Nordås, H. and D. Rouzet (2015), "The impact of services trade restrictiveness on trade flows: First estimates", *OECD Trade Policy Papers*, No. 178, OECD Publishing, Paris, *http://dx.doi.org/10.1787/5js6ds9b6kjb-en*.

OECD (2017), *Key issues for digital transformation in the G20*, Report prepared for a joint German Presidency/OECD Conference, Berlin, January, *www.oecd.org/g20/key-issues-for-digital-transformation-in-the-g20.pdf*.

OECD (2016), "New forms of work in the digital economy", *OECD Digital Economy Papers*, No. 260, OECD Publishing, Paris, *http://dx.doi.org/10.1787/5jlwnklt820x-en*.

Rodrik, D. (2016), "Premature deindustrialization", *Journal of Economic Growth*, Vol. 21, pp. 1-33.

Rouzet, D., S. Benz and F. Spinelli (2017), "Trading firms and trading costs in services", *OECD Trade Policy Papers*, forthcoming.

Rubalcaba, L. and H. Kox (eds.) (2007), *Business services in European economic growth*, Houndmills, Basingstoke, Palgrave MacMillan, Hampshire.

SNA (2008), *United Nations System of National Accounts*, *https://unstats.un.org/unsd/nationalaccount/default.asp*.

Susskind, R. and D. Susskind (2015), *The future of the professions: How technology will transform the work of human experts*, Oxford University Press, Oxford.

Van der Boor, P., P. Oliveira and F. Veloso (2014), "Users as innovators in developing countries: The global sources of innovation and diffusion in mobile banking services", *Research Policy*, Vol. 43, pp. 1594-1607.

Wagner, J. (2012), "International trade and firm performance: A survey of empirical studies since 2006", *Review of World Economics*, Vol. 148, pp. 235-267.

Chapter 2

The regulatory environment
for services

Chapter 2 provides a discussion of services policies, drawing on the STRI indices and database. It starts with a short introduction of the STRI and a brief methodological overview of the project. It then sets out the key STRI findings by country and sector and identifies interlinkages among services along the digital network, the transport and distribution supply chain, market bridging and supporting services and physical infrastructure services. The chapter also presents the reforms to services policies that have been undertaken over the period covered so far by the STRI (2014-16). The analysis is supplemented by short case studies describing concretely how services barriers affect firms' ability to establish and conduct business in foreign countries.

The services sector consists of a broad range of economic activities such as telecommunications, financial services, transport and professional services. These fall under the responsibility of different government entities as well as professional bodies with delegated regulatory authority to control access to, and conduct of, the profession. The diversity and complexity of the services sector is a challenge for trade policy makers and negotiators who need to bring on board the regulatory bodies at home and be responsive to the interests of both the business community and consumers. Domestic regulations in the services sector typically predate the first international trade agreements covering services, and therefore differ considerably across countries, even when pursuing the same objectives. Both the level and the differences in regulation may impose significant costs on foreign services suppliers and protect local incumbents from competition from foreign suppliers and sometimes also from local entrepreneurs.

The Services Trade Restrictiveness (STRI) database and indices bring together comparable information on trade-relevant regulation across sectors and countries, providing a tool for policy makers and others to gain oversight over this complex field. For example, it allows policy makers to design reform options, compare them with global best practice, and assess their likely effects; it helps trade negotiators to identify measures that impede trade; and it provides businesses with information on the requirements that traders must comply with when entering foreign markets. Furthermore, since the STRI is updated annually, it allows the evolution of the services policies over time to be monitored.

Introducing the STRI

The STRI is an evidence-based diagnostic tool that provides an up-to-date snapshot of regulations affecting services trade in 44 countries and 22 sectors, representing over 80% of global services trade (Box 2.1). The STRI suite of tools includes i) a regulatory database compiled by the OECD and based on laws and regulations in force; ii) composite indices, taking values between zero (complete openness to trade and investment) and one (total market closure to foreign services providers), that quantify the measures identified; and iii) an online, interactive policy simulator that allows the user to compare selected countries with one another and to simulate potential policy reforms.

The STRI was launched in 2014, and currently captures information for three consecutive years (2014-16). The policy measures that relate to market access and national treatment refer to what applies on a most favoured nation basis and do not take into account preferential treatment through free trade agreements (FTA). However, existing FTAs, with the exception of the European Single Market, usually do not make commitments that go significantly beyond binding existing practices (Miroudot and Pertel, 2015).

The presentation of the STRI starts with general observations on differences across sectors and countries as far as the level and profile of trade restricting regulations are concerned. The subsequent discussion organises selected services sectors around four clusters of related services: the digital network services (telecommunications, broadcasting

Box 2.1. **The OECD Services Trade Restrictiveness Index**

The STRI regulatory database brings together information from more than 16 000 laws and regulations for 22 sectors in 44 countries. These are the 35 OECD countries and Brazil, China, Colombia, Costa Rica, India, Indonesia, Lithuania, the Russian Federation and South Africa. The information has been compiled by the OECD on the basis of a common methodology agreed by OECD countries. It has been verified and peer reviewed by the OECD countries and shared with the emerging economies. The policy measures in the STRI regulatory database are organised under five policy areas:

- *Restrictions on foreign entry* include information on foreign equity limitations, requirements that management or board of directors must be nationals or residents, foreign investment screening, restrictions on cross-border mergers and acquisitions, capital controls, regulations on cross-border data flows and a number of sector-specific measures.

- *Restrictions on movement of people* include information on entry visa quotas, economic needs tests and duration of stay for foreign natural persons providing services as intra-corporate transferees, contractual services suppliers or independent service providers. These categories are covered by the GATS and have in common that the natural persons are not supposed to seek employment in the host country. This policy area also contains information on recognition of foreign qualifications and licensing in regulated professions.

- *Other discriminatory* measures include discrimination of foreign services suppliers as far as taxes, subsidies and public procurement are concerned, and instances where national standards differ from international standards where relevant.

- *Barriers to competition* include information on anti-trust policy, government ownership of major firms and the extent to which government-owned enterprises enjoy privileges and are exempt from competition laws and regulations. Sector-specific pro-competitive regulation in network industries also falls in this category.

- *Regulatory transparency* includes information on consultations and dissemination prior to laws and regulations entering into force. It also records information on administrative procedures related to establishing a company, obtaining a license or a visa.

The first three cover measures generally related to market access and national treatment, the fourth entails information on pro-competitive regulation (or lack thereof), while the fifth category provides objective information on transparency and administrative procedures. A core set of measures is reported for all sectors, but their specification may differ across sectors. For instance, information on foreign equity limits is included for all sectors, but their settings (including "no limit") may be sector-specific. In addition, certain measures capture the nature and market structure of each sector. For instance, there are a number of measures related to pro-competitive regulation in network industries, matters related to the conditions for obtaining a license for regulated professions, and impediments concerning discrimination of foreign financial services suppliers.

The information in the STRI is standardised so that users can easily find and compare specific policy measures across countries. The STRI database records regulations actually in force. For federal states, where the sector may also be regulated at the sub-federal level, a representative state or province is chosen based on output, population and the location of the largest city.

The STRI indices are derived by aggregating regulations that are potentially trade restricting into a composite measure of restrictiveness. The approach taken to scoring in the STRI is to transform qualitative information on regulation into binary scores. To reconcile the complexity of services trade restrictions with binary scoring, non-binary measures are broken down to multiple thresholds; complementary measures are grouped and scored as zero only if no measures in the bundle are restrictive. Finally, in cases where one restriction renders others irrelevant, those measures that are rendered irrelevant are automatically scored one.

Box 2.1. **The OECD Services Trade Restrictiveness Index** (cont.)

The weighting scheme used for the calculation of the STRI relies on expert judgment. A large number of experts were asked to allocate 100 points among the five policy areas presented above. These are translated into weights by assigning the weight experts allocated to the policy area to each measure that falls under it and correct for differences in the number of measures under the policy areas. The sensitivity of the indices to the weighting scheme has been tested by experimenting with alternatives methodologies. Geloso Grosso et al. (2015) explain the methodology in detail.

Figure 2.1 illustrates the contribution of each policy category to the STRI indices in a hypothetical case where the scores are one on all regulatory measures included in the index, thus indicating the most restrictive regime possible. The Restrictions on foreign entry headings account for the largest share of the indices in all sectors and countries, amounting to about 44% of the overall score. The contributions of Restrictions to movement of people, Barriers to competition and Regulatory transparency are about the same at 15% each. However, there are significant differences between sectors. For instance, in the skilled labour-intensive Professional services sector, the Restrictions to the movement of people category accounts for a significantly larger percentage of the indices (33%). In telecommunications services, a sector subject to network effects and significant economies of scale, barriers to competition amount to 39% of the overall score. In transport services, restrictions on foreign entry contribute more than half of the scores (54%), indicating the importance of market entry barriers particularly for services supplied through commercial establishment in the host country.

Figure 2.1. **Contribution to the STRI indices by policy area**

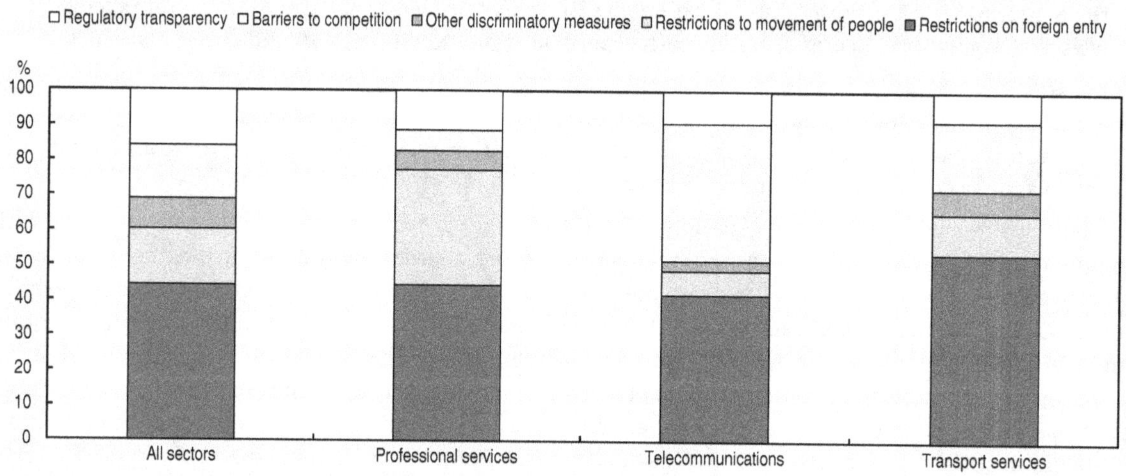

STRI online tools

Several channels disseminate the Services Trade Restriction Index (STRI). The two main data access channels are the STRI internet page and the OECD.Stat repository. The former contains a comprehensive package that includes access to the regulatory database, interactive tools such as Compare Your Country and the policy simulator, a description of the methodology used, and a link to the OECD Trade Policy Papers that deal specifically with STRI.

● **Compare your country** (*www2.compareyourcountry.org/service-trade-restrictions*)

This interactive website can be used to compare services trade restrictiveness across 22 sectors in 44 OECD countries and partner economies. Key economic indicators are projected onto a world map to give a comparative view of the importance of services in the countries covered by the STRI.

> ### Box 2.1. **The OECD Services Trade Restrictiveness Index** *(cont.)*
>
> - **Policy simulator** *(http://sim.oecd.org/)*
>
> The policy simulator provides all STRI information by country and by sector. It can be used to understand how the STRI indices are calculated, to analyse the contribution of each policy measure to the index, to compare countries in detail, and to simulate the impact of a policy change on the index value. The focus view option provides links to legal sources. Finally, simulations can be saved and shared with other users, and the relevant data can be downloaded.
>
> - **Online regulatory database** *(http://qdd.oecd.org/subject.aspx?Subject=STRI)*
>
> The online STRI regulatory database displays complete and up-to-date regulatory information collected for the sector composite indices. This qualitative database contains information on trade restrictions and behind-the-border regulations in the 22 STRI services sectors. Policy measures are categorised under the five policy areas defined above.
>
> The database entries are documented with reference to the sources (title and articles of the relevant law), with an internet link to each legal source. Explanations are provided where answers are ambiguous or to provide greater precision on the context of a specific regulation.
>
> - **Indices can be downloaded from OECD.Stat** *(http://stats.oecd.org/Index.aspx?DataSetCode=STRI)*
>
> The STRI indices are easily accessed and extracted from OECD.Stat (under the heading: Industry and Services, sub heading: Services Trade Restrictions). In addition to the five policy areas, the indices are presented by four additional classifications:
>
> - GATS market access/national treatment and domestic regulation/other
> - GATS modes of supply
> - Discriminatory versus non-discriminatory measures
> - Firm's establishment versus on-going operations
>
> The indices of regulatory heterogeneity based on the same information included in the STRI regulatory database are also displayed under this section.

and computer services), the transport and distribution supply chain services (transport, courier, logistics and distribution services), a market bridging and support services cluster (commercial banking, accounting and legal services) and a physical infrastructure services cluster (construction, architecture and engineering). Together these clusters give an idea of the breadth and variety of sector-specific trade policy measures, and also demonstrate that trade restrictive policy measures in one sector may have an impact on other sectors along services value chains, which in turn may be part of global value chains designing, fabricating and marketing goods.[1]

No sector is fully open – some sectors are completely closed in some countries

The restrictiveness of services trade policies varies substantially across countries within sectors and between sectors as illustrated by Figure 2.2 which shows the average, minimum and maximum index values for each of the 22 sectors included in the STRI database. Bearing in mind that caution is needed when comparing sectors, it is fair to say that air transport, legal services and accounting and auditing services tend to be more restrictive on average than other sectors. Air transport is the only substantial services sector that remains outside the scope of the General Agreement of Trade in Services (GATS) and it is not surprising that it is less open to trade than other services sectors. Note, however, that so far the STRI only covers trade through commercial presence in this sector.[2]

Figure 2.2. **STRI average, minimum and maximum scores by sector, 2016**

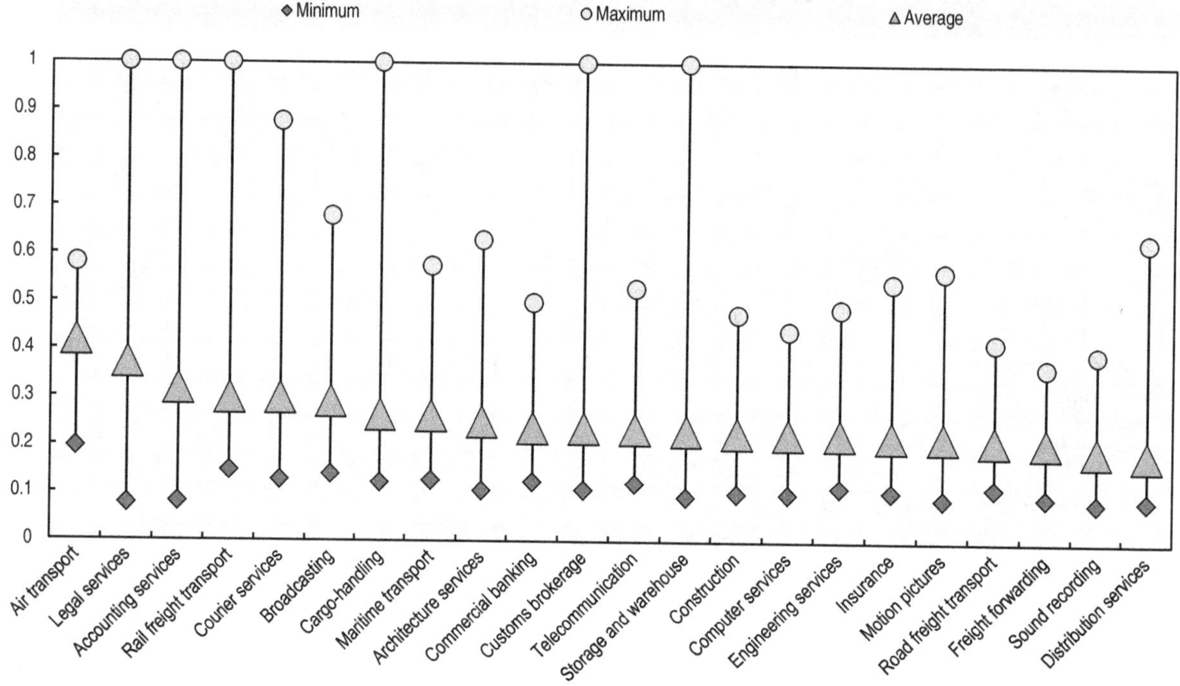

Legal services, auditing and to a lesser extent accounting are regulated professions for which licensed professionals have exclusive rights to provide services. Traditionally, the criteria for obtaining a license have been a degree from a local higher education institution, local practice and in many cases also nationality or citizenship. Although many countries have lifted some of these requirements, elements of such regulatory regimes remain in place, explaining the high average score. Furthermore, a few countries still reserve professional services for local citizens. As noted in the previous chapter, knowledge-intensive business services (KIBS) have embarked on a digital transformation path which makes them tradable, accessible and affordable for consumers as well as SMEs, given that regulation is brought in line with modern technology.

At the other end of the scale, distribution and sound recording (music) services are on average much more open to trade. Yet, in all sectors, there is a large gap between the highest and the lowest score. As documented in Chapter 3, this variation matters not only for the trade performance of the sectors in question, but also for the efficiency of local service provision and the performance in downstream sectors.

On average, developing countries tend to have more restrictive services trade policies than OECD countries. Indeed, a statistically significant negative correlation between the STRI score and GDP per capita is found in all sectors and the relationship is strongest in commercial banking, insurance and telecommunications.[3] Interestingly, these sectors are subject to prudential (i.e. risk-reducing) or pro-competitive regulations in all countries. The level of GDP per capita is closely related to regulatory capacity. Thus, it is conceivable that poorer countries are more cautious in opening their markets due to concerns that foreign entry may overwhelm their regulatory capacity.

While countries at different stages of economic development may have different policy priorities, it is important to note that few, if any, restrictions are unique to emerging economies; most of them are found in some shape or form in OECD countries as well. Indeed, none of the 44 countries so far included in the STRI database is amongst the top three or bottom three in terms of trade restrictiveness in all 22 sectors. All countries in the sample have sectors and policy areas where there is scope for reform, whereas at the same time all countries have areas of good performance that could be a model for others. The STRI indices for all sectors and countries are presented in the annex to this book.

The digital network

The digital supply chain consists of i) content such as audio-visual services, design and other knowledge-capturing products, ii) the capture, compression and ingestion of content into transmission networks, iii) digital rights management and iv) content delivery. Telecommunications and broadcasting provide the networks over which content is delivered, and computer and information services offer a host of services including information storage and processing, network management systems and over-the-top (OTT) services complementing and sometimes competing with telecommunications and broadcasting services.

Recent years have seen convergence of telecommunications, information services and broadcasting where content can be delivered over different networks. Telecommunications operators often offer Internet Protocol Television (IPTV) as part of so-called triple play or quadruple play packages (broadband, television and telephone for triple play, adding mobile for quadruple play), and in some cases broadcasters have become telecommunications operators. In addition to linear broadcasting, video-on-demand has become increasingly important for distribution of audio-visual content. Furthermore, many suppliers are offering streaming or downloads on the Internet. Both IPTV and video-on-demand require access to high-speed broadband and the supply of these services depends on the performance and regulation in the telecommunications sector. By the same token, a vibrant IPTV and video-on-demand market creates demand for broadband internet services. Reflecting this reality, the same regulatory body oversees telecommunications and broadcasting in a number of countries.

Telecommunications and broadcasting are considered to be of strategic importance, prompting many countries to restrict foreigners from investing and operating in these sectors. National control does not necessarily mean limiting access to foreign services providers, however. Best practice policies involve an independent regulator that sets standards in accordance with international standards, monitors the market and enforces pro-competitive regulation, including specific obligations on suppliers with significant market power, be they locally or foreign owned. Trade-restricting measures to ensure national control take several forms of which the most common are foreign ownership limitations, government ownership of major suppliers, screening of foreign investment and requiring that the directors and management of companies are nationals or residents in the country.

In a capital-intensive network industry, access to essential facilities and switching costs may favour incumbent firms. These market imperfections may constitute a substantial entry barrier, even in the absence of explicit foreign entry restrictions. Therefore, pro-competitive regulation is considered a trade policy issue in telecommunications, which is addressed in the WTO Telecommunications Services Reference Paper as well as in a number of regional trade agreements. Lack of pro-competitive regulation is scored as a trade-restricting barrier to competition in the STRI in cases where an incumbent operator has significant market power.

Ex ante pro-competitive regulation is less common for broadcasting, although regulators often take into account convergence between networks and platforms when assessing the market structure and making regulatory decisions in telecommunications markets.

Figure 2.3 plots the STRI score in telecommunications (horizontal axis) and broadcasting (vertical axis) in 2016. Each bubble represents a country and the size of the bubble represents the number of routed autonomous systems (AS) per 100 000 inhabitants. It indicates the ease with which a company may take control over routing its traffic and exchange this traffic with other networks, which may be a good proxy for the level of competition in the market (OECD, 2015a). Three messages can be taken from this graph. First, countries tend to have a similar level of trade restrictions in broadcasting and telecommunications. Second, the emerging economies covered by the STRI appear in the upper right-hand corner of the chart, suggesting that the level of restrictiveness is negatively related to the level of income in the country. However, as demonstrated in Box 2.2, which shows the STRI for telecommunications in Korea over a 20-year period, liberalisation and pro-competitive regulations can evolve over time as the country develops institutional capacity and economic strength.[4] Third, a high level of restrictiveness is associated with fewer autonomous systems.[5]

Figure 2.3. **STRI in telecommunications and broadcasting, 2016**

Openness matters for performance

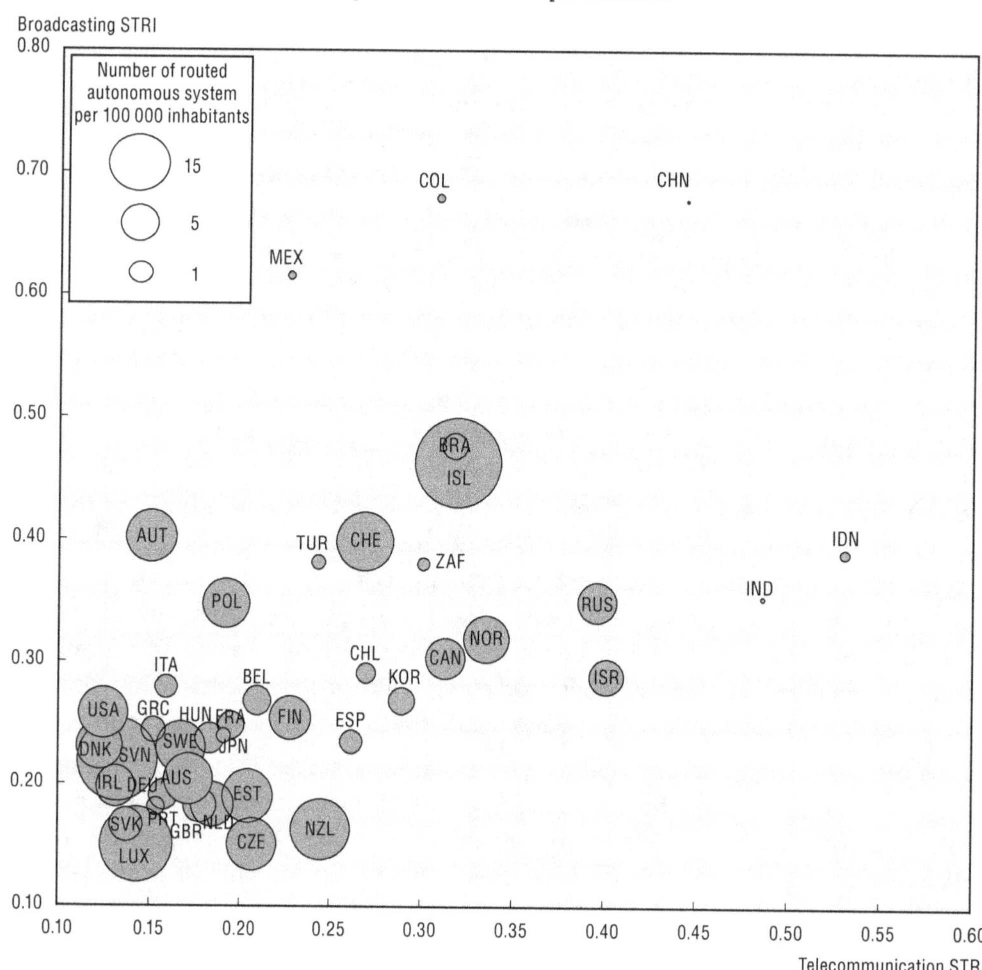

Source: OECD STRI database (2016) and OECD (2015a).

Box 2.2. **Korea's services trade policies over two decades: Telecommunications**

The telecommunications sector in Korea experienced two main waves of reform starting in the late 1990s and in the late 2000s. In the first wave, foreign investment in the sector was substantially liberalised. The foreign equity cap in facilities-based telecommunication businesses was raised from 33% to 49% in 1999, and the ban on foreign investors investing in the Korea Telecommunication Corporation (KTC) was converted into a 33% limit in 1998, raised to 49% in 2001. The requirement that the majority of a facilities-based telecommunication provider's board of directors must be Korean nationals was also removed in 1997, and conditions on cross-border mergers and acquisitions eased in 2001.

During the same period, some reforms towards a more pro-competitive regulatory framework were also implemented, such as mandatory number portability and unbundling of the local loop in 2001. The remaining government stake in KTC was unwound in 2002.

The second wave of reform focused on enhancing the competitive environment and closing the gap with best-practice regulation of dominant players. Between 2008 and 2011, a number of regulatory changes were enacted, including the establishment of an independent Korea Communications Commission, dialling parity, accounting separation, wholesale access conditions and prices, and the resale of public telecommunications services to other suppliers. At the same time, minimum capital requirements for special-category telecommunications were put in place starting in 2008. As of 2015, information on spectrum is made publicly available.

Figure 2.4. **Korea's STRI in telecommunications, 1996-16**

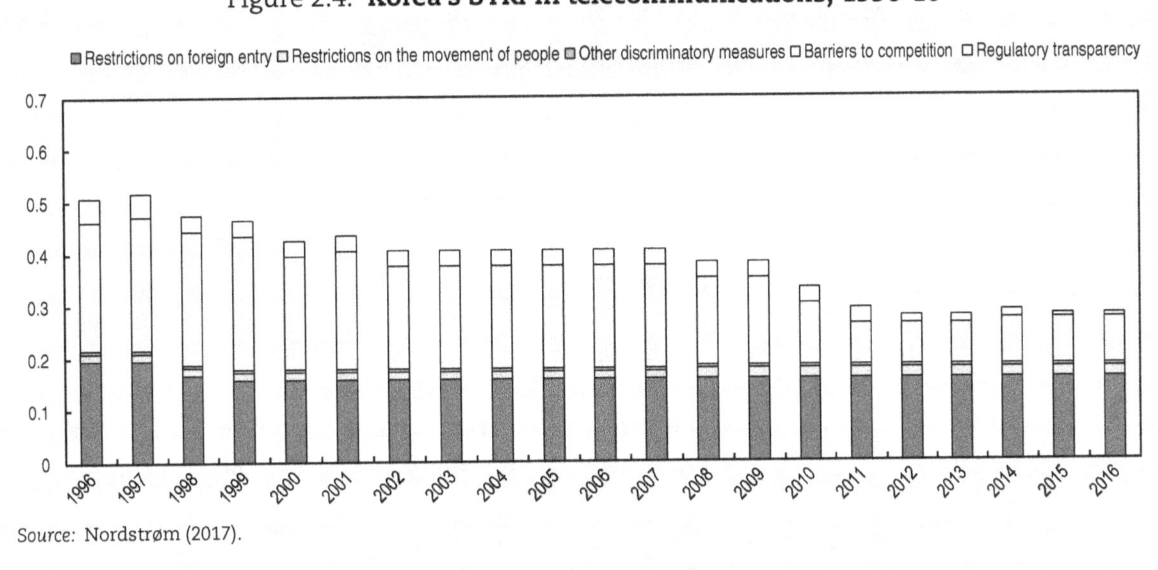

Source: Nordstrøm (2017).

Foreign equity restrictions are quite common in broadcasting, although cable and satellite TV are typically more open to foreign investment than is terrestrial broadcasting. Public ownership of one or more broadcasters or TV channels is also common. Furthermore, state-owned broadcasters often enjoy competitive advantages related to funding or other favourable conditions. In fact, only two countries in the sample have neither foreign equity restrictions nor government ownership of a major TV channel. Turning to limitations on content, some countries require that broadcasters reserve a certain percentage of transmission time excluding news, sports events, advertising, games and teleshopping for local content. A number of countries that have such screen quotas extend this to non-linear demand like streaming for consistency across platforms. In a few countries, there are quotas also on the number of TV channels.

Digital rights management is also covered by the STRI database and indices. Copyright and related rights are integral features of the audio-visual sector, since transactions are essentially the transfer of property rights from a seller to a buyer, or the right to use somebody's intellectual property for a rental or fee. Most countries covered by the STRI database have incorporated compliance with international treaties in their copyright and other IPR legislation, and few discriminate against foreign supplies regarding copyright protection and distribution of license fees. However, this is an area of rapid technical change where implementation and the specifics of regulation are important.

The transport and distribution supply chain

Transport and logistics services are not only extensively traded in their own right but are also intermediate services at the core of global value chains and just-in-time inventory management, with the related demand for door-to-door services. Distribution services are essential for bringing goods from the producer to the consumer, for job creation and for demand-driven economic growth. The rise of online retail sales has led to an increase in parcel delivery, and the importance of global production networks depends on both fast and reliable shipments. As global value chains have become a dominant feature of world trade in recent decades, the concept of transport and logistics services has evolved significantly to cover a wide range of activities for integrated supply management, from network strategy design to the distribution and delivery phases.

The STRI for transport services covers air, maritime, road and rail freight transport. Logistics services complement air cargo, shipping and trucking in the supply chain. In international trade in goods, the process of bringing goods from factory gates across borders and to markets relies heavily on the efficiency of auxiliary services and the speed of carrying out border procedures. In that respect, the STRI covers four types of logistics services: cargo-handling, storage and warehousing, freight forwarding services and customs brokerage.

Air and maritime transport form part of the backbone of merchandise trade, and are important enablers for integration into global value chains. Air transport facilitates particularly the movement of components that have a high value-to-weight ratio and goods that require speedy and reliable transport (for instance, perishable goods). Air transport also facilitates speedy movement of business travellers assisting clients or providing after sales services. Maritime transport, in turn, is crucial for transporting large volumes of cargo at lower costs.

In air transport services, the level of restrictiveness is high across the board. Most countries restrict foreign equity participation in the sector to less than 50%. Notable exceptions include Chile, Colombia, and Costa Rica, which do not apply any limitations on foreign ownership of domestic airlines. As part of a reform package introduced in 2016, India allows foreigners to invest up to 100% in domestic airlines but a 49% limitation remains in place for investments made by foreign airlines. Australia (with the exception of Qantas) and New Zealand also allow 100% foreign ownership in domestic airlines for the purpose of carrying domestic traffic only, whereas Mexico and Japan allow complete foreign ownership in domestic airlines carrying international traffic only. Indonesia allows majority foreign ownership in air freight transport, following recent reforms in its Negative Investment List in 2016. Ownership restrictions are often coupled with specific limitations on the nationality of board members and managers of air carriers. The lease of foreign aircraft with crew ("wet lease") or without crew ("dry lease") is subject to prior authorisation in a large number of countries.

The main impediment to competition in the sector relates to slot allocation at airports for landings and take-offs. Most countries in the STRI database assign slots in high-demand airports based on historical rights – which entails giving preference to incumbent airlines – and typically also forbid the commercial exchange of slots between airlines. However, it is common that, after the allocation of historic slots, half of the remaining slot pool is allocated to new airlines. While this can promote competition, the extent to which it confers a real benefit on new entrants will depend on how many slots are freed up by incumbent airlines.

Maritime transport carries around 80% of merchandise trade by volume. A special feature of this sector is the separation of nationality of ship owners, the registration of the ship and the routes being serviced by the ships. As of 2016, about 71% of all ships (measured by tonnage) owned by the 35 largest ship-owner nations were registered under foreign or international flag. Maritime transport is thus a truly international services sector where cross-border trade is important.

Restrictions on cabotage operations (i.e. traffic between two or more ports within the same country) are predominant, and often combined with restrictions on foreigners owning or registering vessels under the national flag. Ten countries in the STRI database have also signed cargo sharing agreements and five reserve specific types or shares of their domestic cargoes to the national fleet. Ports, which are crucial gateways for cargo flows, are often publicly owned, while port services are provided by private companies operating under concessions. Seven countries still maintain restrictions to the provision of such services, including statutory monopolies precluding the entry of other port operators. A few countries apply discriminatory tariffs for port services and in several countries, domestic shipping companies benefit from tax relief measures or other incentives to further increase the competitiveness of the national fleet. In addition, many countries exempt liner codes from competition law, and a handful of countries reserve the provision of port services to concessions granted with exclusive rights.

Among the four logistics services, cargo handling and customs brokerage have a medium to high overall level of restrictiveness. One country is completely closed both in cargo handling and storage and warehousing as it maintains a statutory monopoly on the provision of these services. Customs brokerage is also completely closed in one country which requires nationality for customs brokers. Barriers to competition are also relevant in cargo-handling services, particularly cross-subsidisation, which is prohibited only in a few countries.

Customs procedures and trade facilitation measures play a significant role in the STRI for cargo-handling services and logistics services. These measures are key for the fast delivery of goods and, hence, for the efficient provision of logistics services. A positive development in this area in recent years has been the creation of a single-window regime, which is found in most countries in the STRI database.[6] The deployment of the single window is valuable for internationally oriented businesses, especially for SMEs. Another important regulation relates to the requirement by different regulatory agencies for an individual license to carry out the different logistics services. This requirement, present in many countries in the STRI database, constrains the provision of integrated, seamless logistics services, which is increasingly the business model nowadays.

With seaborne transport underpinning global trade in goods, logistics services at ports increasingly play a fundamental role in the seamless movement of large-scale cargo. The ability for the supplier of logistics services to handle, store, and forward cargo quickly and efficiently is a major factor in meeting the increasing demand for goods and ensuring an unhindered participation in global value chains. Figure 2.5 shows that the STRIs in cargo-handling and in storage and warehousing services are closely associated with the quality of port infrastructure. The chart also shows that an increased level of restrictiveness in cargo-handling is generally coupled with an increased level of restrictiveness in storage and warehousing. The chart finally suggests a correlation between high scores on the STRI in the two logistics services sectors and the distance to international best performance regarding the quality of port infrastructure.

Figure 2.5. **STRIs in key logistics sectors and quality of port infrastructure, 2016**

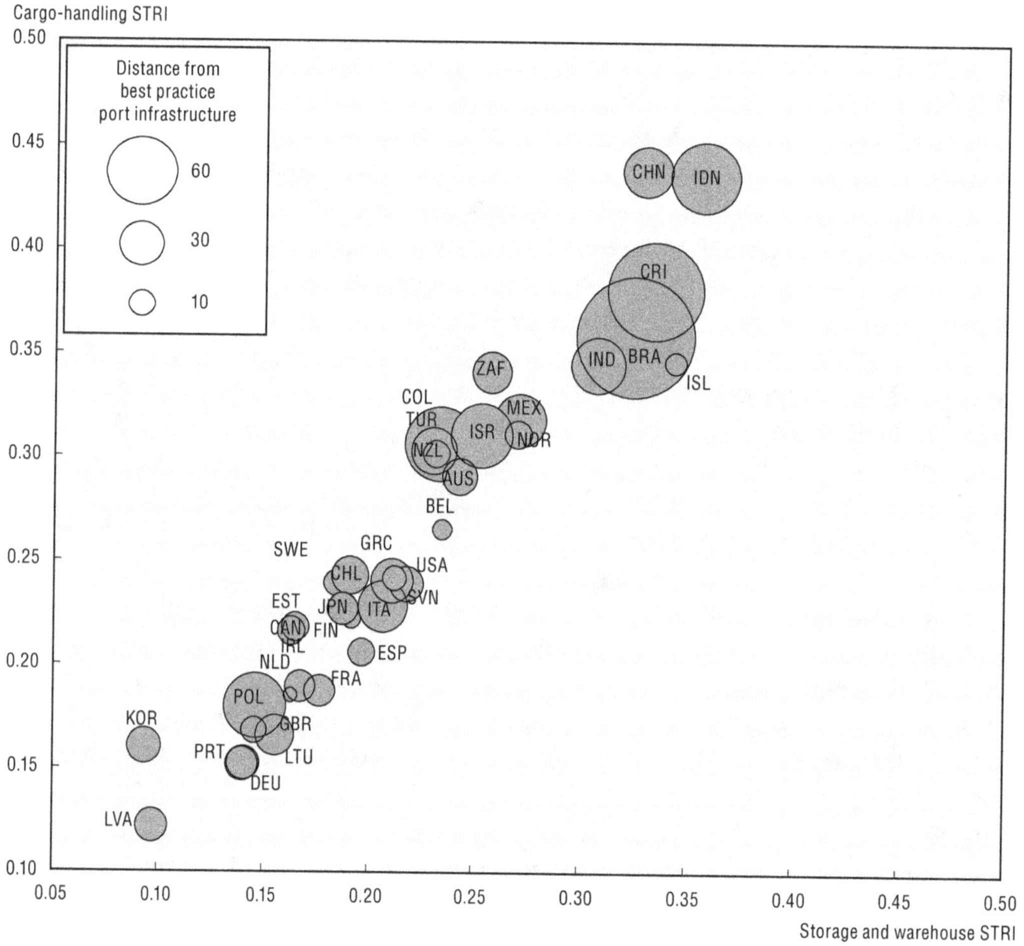

Source: OECD STRI and World Economic Forum (2016).

The STRI results for distribution services, covering wholesale and retail depict a relatively liberal sector. Only two countries restrict foreign equity participation in the retail or wholesale segment. One of them allows 67% foreign ownership in the wholesale segment but foreign investment in retail trade is largely precluded. A number of countries require commercial presence before cross-border distribution services can be supplied. Several countries also require that the distribution of certain products, such as alcoholic beverages at either retail level or wholesale level, be reserved for domestic-owned statutory monopolies.

The market structure of distribution services has been changing rapidly with the emergence of e-commerce and multi-channel retailers (Box 2.3). Restrictions that impede these activities can be found in several countries, including bans on business-to-consumer (B2C) e-commerce. Other impediments include discriminatory access to certain payment settlement methods and the lack of provision for non-resident foreigners to register and declare taxes online. Furthermore, regulations on sales periods and opening hours are common, and a few countries also impose restrictions on the distribution of certain products.

Box 2.3. **How platforms changed the retail sector: the case of eBay**

Founded in 1995, eBay Inc. connects millions of buyers and sellers globally through the eBay Marketplace, StubHub and Classifieds platforms. The technologies and services that power the eBay platforms are designed to enable sellers worldwide to organise and offer their inventory for sale, and buyers to find and purchase it, virtually anytime anywhere. In 2016, the eBay Marketplace saw 162 million active buyers from 190 countries and sellers from around the world.

Online commerce platforms make it possible for firms of all sizes, including micro, small and medium-sized enterprises, to serve an international customer base directly from anywhere. They provide low cost access to services such as international marketing, delivery, payments, and effective communication. A study covering 18 countries found that eBay commercial sellers (i.e. sellers with more than USD 10 000 in sales on eBay) engaged in cross-border transactions reach, on average, 27 different countries in a year (eBay, 2016a). To put this in context, in the majority of OECD countries, 50% or more of exporting enterprises trade with only one country (OECD, 2015b).

Online platforms such as eBay also allow firms to adapt more easily to changes in demand. For example, during the recent economic and financial crisis, companies in general attempted to rebalance their export destinations in response to the significant decrease in demand in Europe (EU, 2015). Large firms were more adaptable and flexible than MSMEs, expanding extra-EU exports by 26% over the period 2009 to 2013. However, EU eBay Commercial Sellers (the majority of which are micro-sized) were by far the most adaptable, increasing their share of extra-EU exports by 52% (eBay, 2016b).

Market bridging and supporting services

Economic activity in general and international transactions in particular rely heavily on access to credit, payment systems and insurance. A legal framework supporting the enforcement of contracts is one of the most important pillars of a market economy in which strangers can do business with each other. Trustworthy, transparent and easy to understand accounting information is needed in order to assess the creditworthiness of strangers. With the growing complexity of international business, these services are essential for entrepreneurs to develop and commercialise their ideas, for the functioning of value chains, and for investors to contribute to growth and innovation. As discussed in greater depth in Chapter 1, digitisation has made these services more easily tradable over digital networks using platforms, clouds and dedicated software. The digital transformation has made them more accessible and affordable for SMEs and consumers. Finally, financial services are important for the transition from an economy based largely on informal economic activities to activities with access to legal enforcement of contracts and protection of worker's rights and other benefits.

However, regulation has not always kept up with technology and there is ample scope for reforms that would strike a better balance between protecting consumers and enabling a more open and competitive market for professional and financial services. Figure 2.6 depicts the STRI for legal services on the horizontal axis and commercial banking on the vertical axis. Each bubble represents a country and the size of the bubble reflects new business registrations per 1 000 people aged 15-64. Three messages can be taken from this graph. First, commercial banking enjoys a less restrictive policy environment than legal services. Second, countries with relatively low scores on the STRI in both sectors (towards the lower-left corner) have more business start-ups. Finally, it is noted that some countries have low business start-up rates in spite of relatively open markets for financial and professional services, suggesting that access to finance and legal advice is not enough to unleash entrepreneurial spirits.

Figure 2.6. **STRI in legal services and commercial banking, 2016**
Openness matters for entrepreneurship

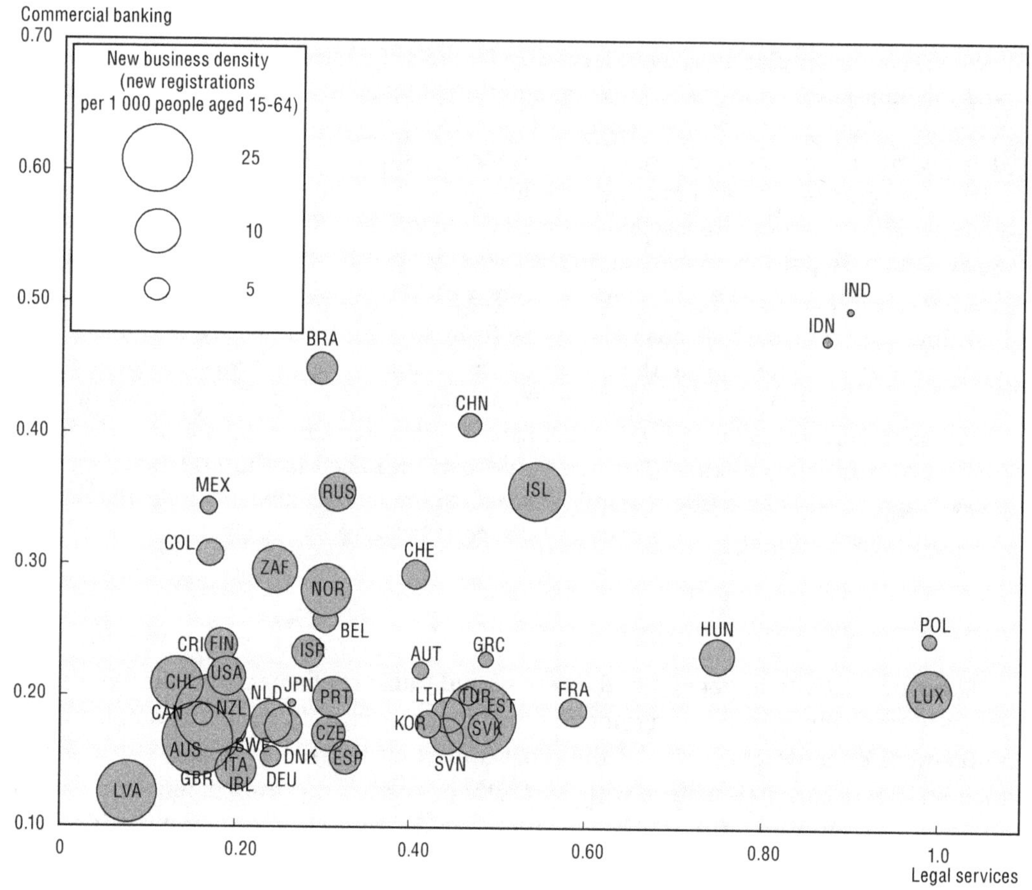

Source: OECD STRI and WDI.

Legal services are typically highly regulated through professional bodies that issue licenses, monitor conduct of professionals and set and uphold professional standards. Among the countries covered by the STRI, four countries reserve both domestic and international legal practice to licenced national lawyers and require that only licensed lawyers form and own law firms. In one of them, there is an opportunity for foreign legal services providers to do business through business visits to provide legal advice to their clients (fly-in-fly-out), another allows foreign lawyers to work for local advocates to advise on foreign law, while in two other countries, the sector is completely closed to lawyers from third countries that are not covered by a common market agreement or mutual recognition. Although most countries have elements of this type of regulation for domestic law, what makes these two countries stand out is the lack of liberalisation regarding international law practice, which is at least partially open in the other 41 countries in the STRI.

The requirements for obtaining a licence to practice and the activities reserved for licensed professionals largely define market access for foreign suppliers of legal services. Domestic law has traditionally played a marginal role in international trade in legal services due to qualification requirements which, like domestic law, are shaped along national lines. Best-practice regulation in this area entails the establishment of a process that provides for substantive criteria (e.g. theoretical and practical aspects of legal training) and administrative procedures (e.g. processing time and right of appeal) for recognising education degrees gained in foreign countries (see Box 2.2 for the case of Canada). In three countries covered in the STRI database, Finland, Latvia and Sweden, licensed lawyers do not have exclusive rights to provide services and appear in court.

Like legal services, accounting services are also intensive users of skilled labour and subject to licensing in a majority of countries. However, in 19 countries covered by the STRI, accounting is not a regulated profession. Foreign equity limits are rarely applied, although some countries restrict firms' ownership to locally licensed professionals. Ownership restrictions are often coupled with requirements that the majority of the board (or equity partners in the case of partnerships) be locally licensed. Foreign accountants tend to be subject to economy-wide limitations on natural persons wishing to provide services in another country on a temporary basis as intra-corporate transferees, contractual services suppliers or independent services suppliers. In addition, nationality and residency requirements to practice in the host country, coupled with the lack of recognition of foreign qualifications can amount to significant constraints on the ability of accountants to provide services.

Along with accounting, the STRI also covers auditing. This profession is subject to licensing in all but one country in the STRI database. Hence, the requirements for obtaining a license to practice and the activities reserved for licensed professionals largely define market access for foreign suppliers. In cases where only nationals can obtain a license and a license is required to practice and to hold shares in auditing or accounting firms, market access for foreign suppliers is very limited. When these regulations apply to both accounting and auditing services, and are coupled with non-availability of temporary licensing as an additional channel for entry into the market, the sector is completely closed. This is the case for the two countries in the sample which has an STRI score of one.

Commercial banking has a relatively high level of trade restricting regulations on average across countries, and the dispersion from the highest to the lowest is relatively narrow (Figure 2.1). This can be explained by the fact that banking is a heavily regulated sector for the purpose of maintaining the stability and soundness of the financial system. Prudential rules and standards are set by national governments and regulators as well as international financial standard-setting bodies.[7] Many countries resort to trade-restricting measures to protect the financial system. Only two countries covered by the STRI impose limits on foreign equity in this sector, but most require a commercial presence to allow cross-border banking and several countries restrict the establishment of foreign bank branches or impose more stringent requirements to grant a license to foreign-owned banks than domestic ones. In most cases, foreign banks must be locally established in order to provide the full range of services in the country. Another common impediment is the requirement that the majority of the board of directors' members of a commercial bank be a domestic national or permanent resident.

Government ownership is also widely observed in the sector. This is often a result of government bailouts during the financial crisis where most countries are yet to re-privatise the bailed out banks. Product-level regulations, including price restrictions and prior approval requirements for individual financial products, are also significant contributions to the STRI indices, particularly in non-OECD member countries. Another common issue is the lack of independence of the regulatory and supervisory authorities. Indeed, in many countries full operational, management and budget independence from the government is not guaranteed.

Box 2.4. **Requalifying as local lawyers in Canada**

In order to obtain a full licence to practise law in any Canadian province or territory, foreign lawyers must apply to the National Committee on Accreditation (NCA) for evaluation of their credentials and experience. The NCA establishes the educational and practising criteria an applicant must meet to be considered for admission to any of the law societies. Upon successful completion of this assessment, which is made before the foreign lawyers apply for admission to the bar in Canada, the NCA issues a Certificate of Qualification.

The NCA applies a harmonised standard on a national basis so that applicants outside Canada do not need to satisfy different entrance standards to practise law in the different provinces and territories. Each application is assessed on an individual basis, taking into account the specific elements of each applicant's educational and professional background (e.g. the type of legal system and the subject areas studied, whether the legal education programme is recognised by the local regulatory authority and professional legal experience).

Once an application has been assessed by the NCA, a candidate may be asked to complete specific law school courses and to pass examinations to demonstrate competence in specific subject areas. The requirements that are assigned focus on the competence of applicants in core common law subjects of Canadian law (e.g. administrative law, constitutional law and criminal law). Other subject areas not specific to Canadian law (e.g. commercial law or civil procedures) may be recognised, depending on the candidate's education and experience.

The NCA processes applications in the order they are received by the Federation of Law Societies of Canada. An applicant will normally receive an assessment report within eight weeks from the time that all required formalities have been completed. Applicants may appeal the assessment issued by the NCA by submitting a letter to the NCA indicating the reasons for the appeal. An Appeal Panel established by the NCA considers the appeal and issues its decision, which may reduce or supplement the requirements set out in the decision being appealed.

Physical infrastructure services

Physical infrastructure services include construction, architecture and engineering services. Construction services have historically been considered strategic for providing the infrastructure for other industries as well as due to its close links to public works and the allocation of fiscal resources. Architects undertake the design of buildings whereas engineers participate in the construction of key infrastructure such as buildings, roads and bridges. Often engineering and architectural activities are combined in projects offered by one company, and are sometimes subsumed in the construction sector. Engineers are also important for the development of production processes and the adoption of new technologies throughout the economy.

The complementarity between architecture, engineering and construction is reflected in the regulation of the sectors where countries take different approaches to which links in the chain to regulate and how. In 17 countries covered in the STRI, engineering is not a regulated profession, whereas for architecture eight countries adopt a similar approach. This does not necessarily mean that there is less government control during the process of designing and constructing a building, a road or other infrastructure projects. Rather, some countries consider strong enforcement of object-related regulation, such as building codes, technical and safety standards sufficient to achieve safety and other social objectives.

In the construction sector, the more elevated levels of restrictiveness can largely be attributed to general measures affecting all sectors of the economy. This includes impediments on acquiring land and real estate, which typically have a direct bearing on the provision of construction services. For example, property developers may not be able to own real estate under construction until completion of the project. There are 24 countries in the STRI database which have restrictions in this area.

Construction services are a relatively labour-intensive sector (both skilled and unskilled), which is typically reflected in a higher share in employment than in GDP for most countries. Given the nature of construction activities, the potential for mechanisation and automation, and therefore capital-intensive production, remains limited. Restrictions on the movement of people thus have a significant impact on the indices for the sector. Apart from labour market tests and other horizontal restrictions, the movement of qualified construction personnel may be affected by licensing and related issues, including lack of recognition of foreign qualifications. In most countries covered in the STRI database, at least one engineer must be locally licensed for the issuance of construction permits.

In light of the importance of government demand for these services, restrictions in public procurement have a particular bearing on the construction sector. A large number of countries limit non-discriminatory access to public procurement to free trade agreements or to WTO Government Procurement Agreement (GPA) partners. Explicit preferences to local suppliers in procurement markets, particularly through price preferences or the use of offsets, are also common. Figure 2.7 shows that the STRI scores for construction services are closely correlated to those for engineering services. Considering that these services are often supplied by the same firms, restrictive policies in complementary sectors lead to joint effects that may impose a heavy toll on services suppliers. Furthermore, Figure 2.7 also shows that the costs of dealing with the procedures needed to obtain a construction permit tend to be more significant in economies with relatively higher score in both sectors, although some exceptions exist.

Engineering is a knowledge-intensive business service. In the 27 countries in which engineering is a regulated profession, foreign professionals may face costly and time-consuming procedures related to licensing and recognition of qualifications. When licensing is combined with residency or nationality requirements in order to obtain a license, access to the market for foreign nationals is very limited. Only one country in the

Figure 2.7. **STRIs in construction and engineering services and costs of dealing with construction permits, 2016**

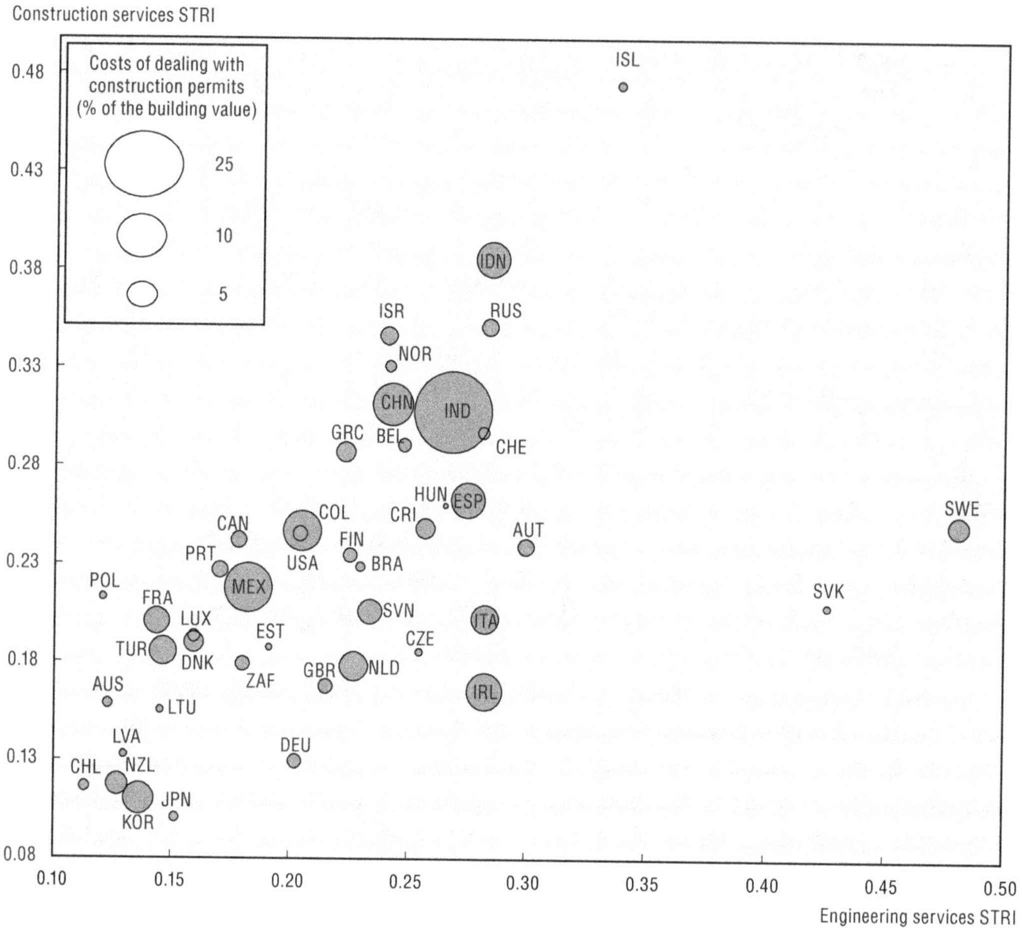

Source: OECD STRI and WB Doing Business Indicators.

STRI database restricts foreign equity in engineering services. In some of the other economies, the majority of shareholders in engineering firms must be licensed professionals. Other impediments relate to restrictions on acquiring land and real estate, and participating in public procurement, which may be particularly pernicious for engineering services given their complementarity with the building industry.

Engineering services are not limited to the building industry. They are also a vital input in the process of gaining competitiveness in high-technology products. Manufacturers employ engineering services through several channels, including hiring engineers for in-house provision of engineering services, and sourcing from local and international engineering firms. Many activities in the sector have been digitalised in recent years, substantially transforming the sector as discussed in Chapter 1.

Reforms of services policies in the STRI (2014-16)

The reforms collected in the STRI reflect changes in the trade policy framework that lead to changes in the answers recorded in the STRI databases. This section presents the main policy changes recorded in the STRI between 2014 and 2016 as well as the effect of these reforms on the indices.

Main reforms

Indonesia introduced significant reforms in 2016 when it updated its Negative Investment List, the main instrument governing foreign investment in the country. The most important reform was to liberalise foreign investment by lifting limitations on foreign equity in a number of service sectors. In telecommunications services, foreign participation in internet communication companies was raised from 49% to 67%, and in fixed and mobile telephone companies from 65% to 67%. The amended list fully opened motion pictures and sound recording to foreign investment. Liberalisation in the air transport sector entailed increasing the limit for foreign participation to 67% from a previous 49%. Segments of logistics services (cargo-handling, storage and warehousing, and freight forwarding) have been liberalised as well: 67% foreign participation is now permitted in all three segments instead of the previous 49% in cargo-handling and freight forwarding, and 33% in storage and warehousing services.

Figure 2.8 shows the changes in Indonesia's STRIs between 2014 and 2016. It shows there was a decrease in the indices of several sectors in 2016 as a result of the updated Negative Investment List. The greatest effect was in motion pictures and sound recording, where the elimination of foreign equity limits almost halved the indices in both sectors. The decrease is less significant in other sectors since foreign equity continues to be capped, although at a higher level than before the 2016 amendments.

Figure 2.8. **Policy reforms in Indonesia, 2014-16**

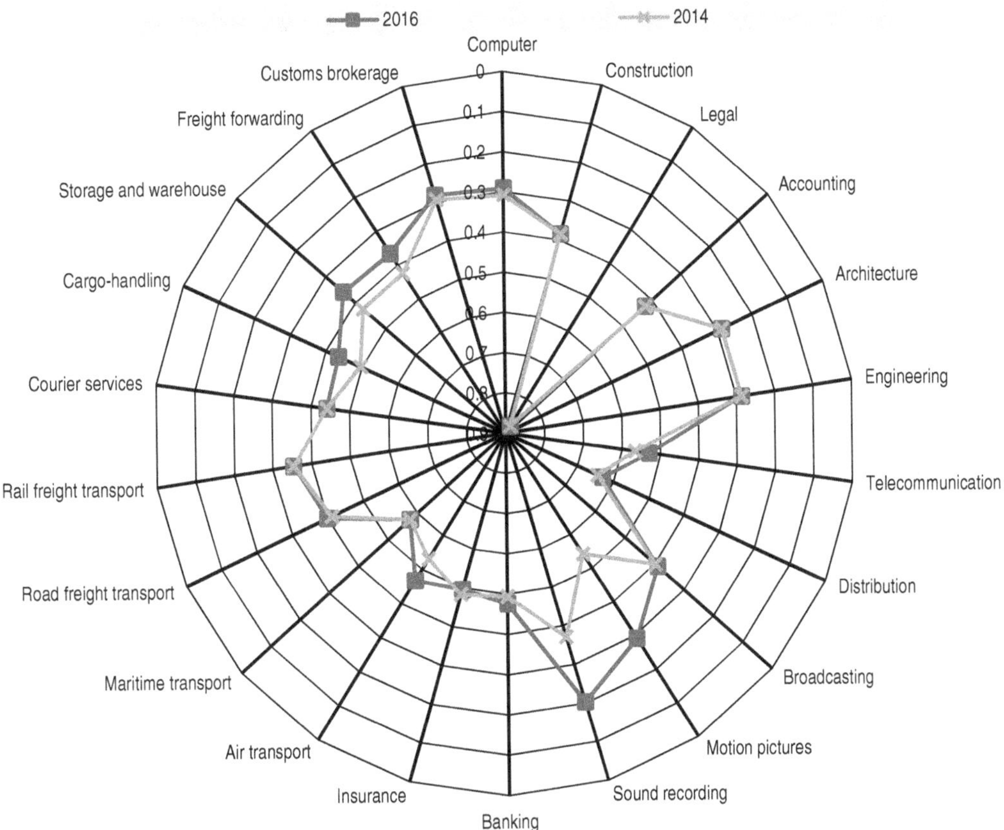

The **People's Republic of China** (hereafter "China") revised the Catalogue for the Guidance of Foreign Investment Industries in 2015. The Catalogue is the main instrument governing foreign direct investment. Industries not listed in the Catalogue are deemed to be open for unrestricted foreign investment. Industries covered by the Catalogue are separated into three categories: encouraged, restricted, and prohibited. In the revised Catalogue, rail freight transportation services and services related to direct sales, including online sales, were removed from the restricted category, thereby allowing full foreign ownership. In telecommunications services, China introduced pro-competitive regulations and revised the Telecom Business Classification Catalogue to allow the resale of mobile communication services. Furthermore, the revised Catalogue introduced more liberal policies towards e-commerce.

In **India,** policies on foreign investment are published in the "Consolidated FDI Policy", which is updated annually. The 2014 edition of the Consolidated FDI Policy raised the foreign equity cap for telecommunications companies from 74% to 100%, although investment above 49% remained subject to Government approval. In 2015, policy reforms particularly targeted the insurance services sector. As an initial step, foreign participation was raised from 26% to 49%. The Insurance Laws (Amendment) Act of 2015 allowed foreign reinsurers to open branch offices in India and set out the conditions for their operation. In 2016, the Consolidated FDI Policy eased the conditions on foreign investment in broadcasting services (i.e. Direct-to-Home (satellite), digital cable networks and so-called Headend-in-the-Sky services (HITS) – a satellite-based system to deliver TV channels to cable operators) by raising foreign participation from 74% to 100%. As an addendum to the FDI Policy, the Government also liberalised investment in air transport companies, except for investment made by foreign airlines, in which case, the threshold remained at 49%.

Mexico adopted a package of reforms, including *inter alia* new legislation in sectors such as telecommunications, broadcasting and financial services. In 2015, a new telecommunications and broadcasting law (*Ley Federal de Telecomunicaciones y Radiodifusión*) entered into force rolling back foreign equity restrictions in fixed-line and internet services segments of the sector. The law also introduced a new independent regulator and a series of pro-competitive measures to challenge the dominant position of incumbent telecommunications firms. With respect to broadcasting services, foreign investment in local corporations remains possible only on the basis of reciprocity whereas other limitations on the broadcast time and discriminatory subsidies were introduced in the new law. The financial reform aimed at strengthening prudential regulation, increasing credit penetration and promoting competition. The reform also allowed foreign financial institutions to open up branches in Mexico for the provision of insurance services.

Less sweeping policy changes relevant to the STRI also took place in other countries:

- Norway adopted the EU postal directive, in 2015, which entailed eliminating the postal monopoly for letters, and introducing other liberalising measures relating to the conditions for operation and access to the postal network.

- Greece lifted the requirement for prior approval for foreign investors to acquire shares in publicly-controlled firms in some service sectors as well as removing fee regulations for professional services (although recommendations on minimum fees remain in place for accountants) in 2014.

- Hungary introduced a decree in 2015 setting out quotas on the number of non-EU nationals that can be granted work permits in the country.

- Japan lifted residency requirements for board members of a domestic corporation in 2015. In 2016 it also strengthened the measures to prevent the transfer of criminal proceeds to fully comply with the best-practice recommendation of Financial Action Task Force on Money Laundering.

- In Korea, the requirement that foreign investors must transfer stocks to Korean national(s) within six months in cases where their registration is cancelled was lifted in 2015. Restrictions on internet banking were also removed. On the other hand, a requirement that only licensed architects may establish an architect firm was introduced.

- The Russian Federation introduced limitations on foreigners' participation in the total authorised capital of credit institutions and reduced the permitted share of foreign equity in broadcasting companies in 2016.

- South Africa eliminated quotas for contractual services suppliers and independent services suppliers, and also repealed labour market tests for intra-corporate transferees in 2014.

- Turkey adopted a regulation in 2015 that implemented the 2013 Law on Liberalisation of the Turkish Rail Transport. The new regulation filled some gaps and paved the way for operationalising the reforms planned for the rail transport sector. In 2016, Turkey also adopted a new law on the protection of personal data.

- In the United States, as of July 2016, foreign banks with USD 50 billion or more in US assets must form a US intermediate holding company to act as the parent company of all of the foreign bank's subsidiaries in the United States.

The extent of policy changes in the STRI

The STRI recorded 140 relevant policy changes between 2014 and 2016 across all countries covered (Figure 2.9). Close to half of the reforms took place in 2015, and one-third in 2016. Most reforms affected regulations that apply across the economy (horizontal measures) while most sector-specific reforms occurred in the telecommunications, financial services (insurance and commercial banking), and broadcasting services sectors.

Some policy changes have a more substantial effect on the STRI than others. Figure 2.10 shows the aggregate change in the scores in each STRI sector where reforms occurred. In both years, the decrease in the scores is greater than the increase. This indicates that, in general, the policy shift has moved towards trade liberalisation. However, there have been some sectors such as broadcasting services and some professional services, where the change has shifted the overall picture in the opposite direction.

Horizontal changes (i.e. common across all sectors) contributed both to increasing as well as decreasing the scores. On the one hand, common trade liberalising changes included improvements on the conditions for foreign firms' establishment and operation by means of removal of minimum capital requirements for registering limited liability companies or corporations, the lifting of residency requirements for board of directors, and the elimination of conditions on capital transfers, among others. Furthermore, improvements in administrative procedures contributed to a lower STRI in various sectors. On the other hand, more stringent regulations on labour market tests and shorter permitted durations of stay for natural persons providing services temporarily as intra-corporate transferees, contractual services suppliers or independent services suppliers, represented the main reason behind horizontal increases in the STRI scores.

Figure 2.9. **Policy changes in the STRI, 2014-16**

Figure 2.10. **Change in scores by sector, 2014-16**

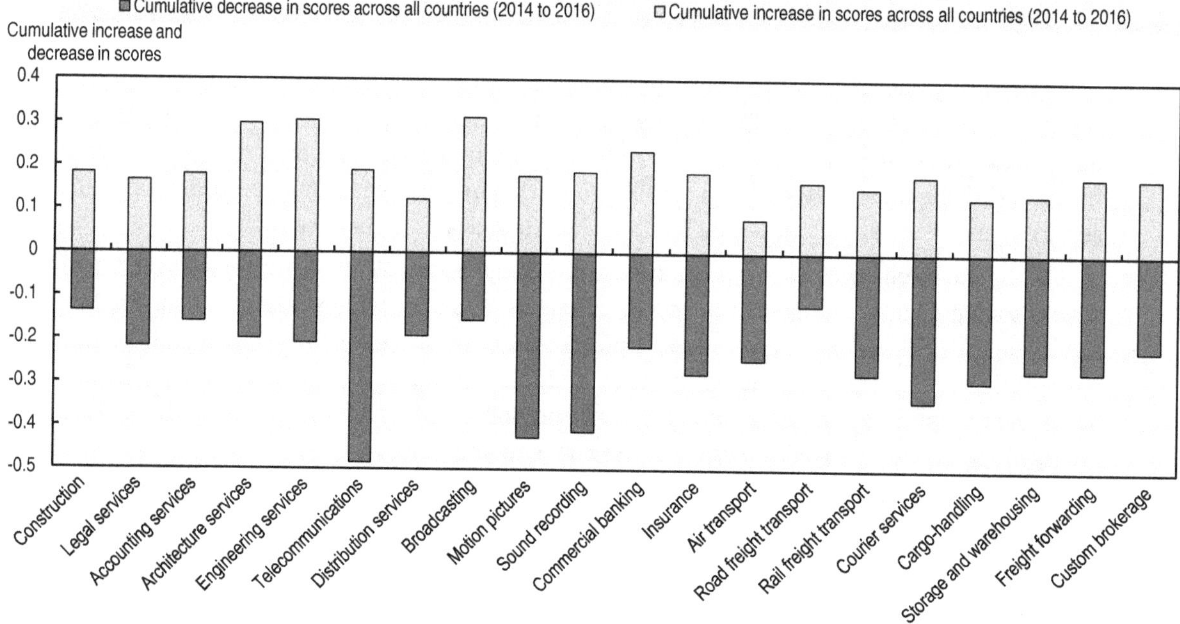

Telecommunications, audio-visual services (broadcasting, motion pictures, sound recording), some professional services, courier services, and logistics services (cargo-handling, storage and warehousing and freight forwarding) have been most affected by sector specific changes. In telecommunications, the main drivers behind the change were the easing of barriers to foreign investment and introducing pro-competitive *ex ante* regulation for dominant suppliers. In audio-visual services, changes in the scores were largely due to changing conditions on foreign participation in audio-visual companies. The increase in professional services stems from horizontal limitations on temporary movement of services suppliers. Due to the knowledge-intensive nature of these services, barriers on movement of people have a higher impact on trade. In courier services, the elimination of conditions on operation and improvement of the competition environment have contributed to the changes. In logistics services, the less restrictive foreign equity limitations have contributed to better indices in cargo-handling, storage and warehousing and freight forwarding services.

Regulatory trade frictions

Services exporters must comply with the regulations in all countries they trade with, and facing a different set of regulatory requirements in each market may add to their cost of doing business.[8] The STRI regulatory heterogeneity indices capture such differences by country pair and sector (Box 2.5)

Box 2.5. **How large are regulatory differences?**

The detail of the STRI database provides information not only on the level of restrictions in force in each country, but also on the extent to which regulatory systems in different markets resemble each other. Indices of regulatory heterogeneity are constructed by comparing countries pairwise, measure by measure and sector by sector. For each measure, the country pair has a score of one if both countries have the same answer (similar regulation) and zero if they have different answers (diverging regulation). The scores are aggregated using the same weights as for the STRI indices, yielding a regulatory heterogeneity index for each country pair in each sector (Figure 2.11).

Figure 2.11. **Regulatory heterogeneity in services, 2016**

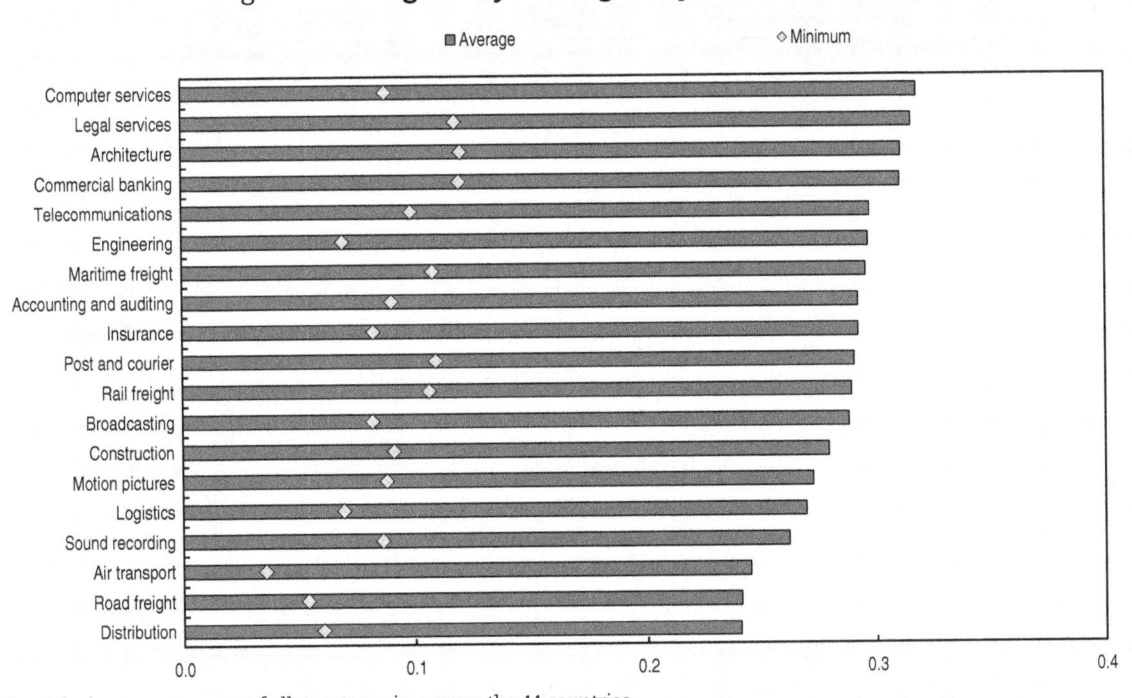

Note: The bars are averages of all country pairs among the 44 countries.
Source: OECD STRI database.

Box 2.5. **How large are regulatory differences?** (*cont.*)

Approaches to regulation differ most across countries in computer services (mostly capturing horizontal regulation), professional services, banking and telecommunications. In these sectors, with the possible exception of the IT industry, regulatory systems were largely established before the advent of new technologies and trade liberalisation turned the markets from local to global.

From 2014 to 2016, the most significant convergence is observed in the telecommunications sector – one of the few sectors for which trade agreements often entail binding commitments on pro-competitive regulation – but also in financial services, audio-visual services, accounting and auditing services. Conversely policy changes have led to a significant divergence in regulation in road freight transport, engineering and computer services (Figure 2.12). It is too early to assess whether divergence over this short period is due to widening regulatory differences or if it is a temporary phenomenon as countries implement reforms at a different pace.

Figure 2.12. **Convergence and divergence in regulation, 2014-16**

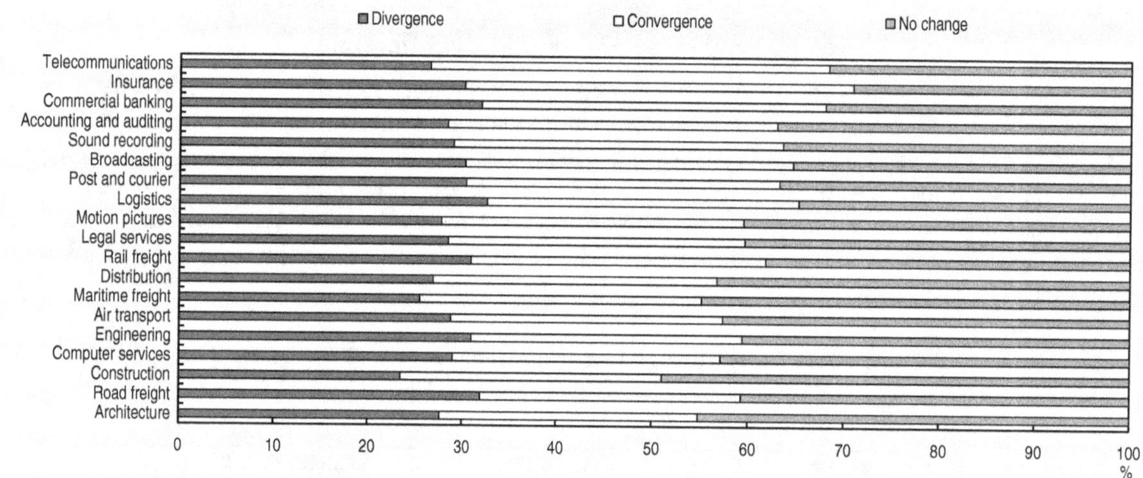

Note: The bars represent the share of all country pairs where the regulatory heterogeneity indices have decreased, stayed constant or increased between 2014 and 2016.
Source: OECD STRI database.

Network graphs are a simple way of visualising the complexity of regulatory heterogeneity across countries and sectors. Network graphs are mathematical structures used to model pairwise links between objects. They are made up of vertices or nodes, which are connected by edges or arrows. The network graphs presented in Figure 2.13 show connections between countries with the most similar regulation, based on the STRI heterogeneity index for the four clusters analysed in this chapter. The size of each country node is measured by its similarity to all other countries. The centrality of countries is indicated by darker shades of blue. Arrows point towards the most similar countries from the perspective of the country from which the arrow originates. The thickness of the lines indicates the degree of bilateral similarity. All countries are assigned at least one arrow to the most similar country. Beyond that, the number of arrows is determined by the number of countries with which the country has a lower than average bilateral heterogeneity index.

A quick glance at the charts suggests that the regulatory heterogeneity indices may be related to distance between countries. Indeed, the correlation between the regulatory heterogeneity index of a country pair and the geographical distance between them is

Figure 2.13. **Regulatory heterogeneity visualised with network graphs for the four STRI sector clusters, 2016**

positive and statistically significant.[9] A common feature in all four charts is one or more clusters of mainly European countries. This is unsurprising since the European Union not only shares a common market, but also has a common regulatory framework for telecommunications, transport, audio-visual services and commercial banking, and the services directive covers most of the other sectors.[10] The highest degree of bilateral similarity is found between the Czech and the Slovak Republics, which in the recent past was the same country; and between France and the Netherlands. The countries that tend to have a distinct regulatory profile across all sectors are Indonesia, China and Brazil, which are found with a small node at the fringe in all four charts.

The four charts also show interesting differences across sectors. The digital network chart shows a large core of relatively similar countries, with a fringe of countries having a more distinct regulatory profile. The transport and distribution supply chain chart is less concentrated, with a cluster of mainly European countries, but also two smaller clusters around the Nordic countries and Australia/New Zealand respectively. However, Denmark is closer to continental Europe than the other Nordic countries in all four charts. The bridging and support services chart depicts a circular network with one major satellite and some outliers with distinct regulatory profiles. The most central countries in the circular network are the Czech Republic, Finland and Lithuania. The satellite to which Japan and Canada/United States are connected is centred on the Netherlands. Finally, the physical infrastructure services chart displays a much more dispersed pattern with smaller clusters. The smallest cluster contains the United States and Canada, being somewhat similar but distinct from the other countries. In the European Union, the professions are regulated (or not) at the national level, subject to a directive on mutual recognition, which is why there is no distinct European cluster in these sectors.

Concluding remarks

The STRI aims at capturing the trade restrictiveness of regulation. In sectors where regulation is necessary for anti-trust purposes, the STRI captures the trade restrictiveness due to lack of regulation. The STRI indices are not meant to be normative, but rather to describe the situation in a given year. It is clear that capacity to adopt best practice evolves over time with experience and resources available to the regulatory bodies. Furthermore, best-practice regulations ensuring that legitimate social objectives are met without restricting international trade themselves evolve as technology brings new services into international markets and provides new tools both for informing and protecting consumers, and for monitoring conduct of services suppliers. The STRI tools are designed to keep up with such changes. They are and will always be work in progress. Reforms must be based on an assessment of costs and benefits of proposed changes. Chapter 3 summarises OECD work on estimating the costs of trade restricting regulations.

Notes

1. See Chapter 3 for further discussion of the link between goods and services.

2. Cross-border trade is governed by a network of bilateral agreements. Work is under way to cover these as well. The same applies to road transport.

3. The pairwise Pearson correlation coefficients range from -0.21 in road transport to -0.67 in commercial banking, with insurance and telecommunications also above 0.6 (in absolute value). The road transport coefficient is statistically significant at the 2% significance level, all others at the 0.1% level or better.

4. The time series of STRIs in selected sectors for Korea come from a recent country-study (OECD, 2017).

5. A common observation for all sectors is that Iceland is an outlier with relatively high scores on the STRI, but which still exhibits a good performance with respect to the sectoral performance indicators shown in this section. A possible explanation for this is that Iceland is a very small economy and a member of the European Economic Area which makes it open to a region that is about 1 000 times its size measured by GDP.

6. A discussion on the development of single windows, and of trade facilitation more generally can be found in Moïsé and Sorescu (2016), which discusses evidence from the OECD Trade Facilitation Indicators covering 163 countries.

7. It should be noted that the STRI does not seek to define the scope or nature of what measures would be considered prudential, but aims to record in an objective and comparable manner the state of legal and regulatory impediments faced by foreign banks.

8. See Nordås (2016) for a full description of the methodology and the indices.

9. The pairwise correlation coefficient is 0.5 and statistically significant at a 0.1% level.

10. EU directives leave some space for member countries to incorporate them into their own legal frameworks and the details may differ somewhat across EU members.

References

eBay (2016a), "Small online business growth report: Towards an inclusive global economy", eBay Public Policy Lab., *www.ebaymainstreet.com/sites/default/files/ebay_global-report_vf_no-countries_0.pdf*.

eBay (2016b), "Platform-enabled small businesses and inclusive economic opportunities", eBay Public Policy Lab., *www.ebaymainstreet.com/sites/default/files/ebay_report_pesbieo_.pdf*.

EU (2015), "Annual report on European SMEs 2014/2015: SMEs start hiring again", *SME Performance Review 2014/2015*, Final Report, available at: *http://ec.europa.eu/growth/tools-databases/newsroom/cf/itemdetail.cfm?item_id=8557*.

Geloso Grosso, M., F. Gonzales, S. Miroudot, H. Kyvik Nordås, D. Rouzet and A. Ueno (2015), "Services Trade Restrictiveness Index (STRI): Scoring and weighting methodology", *OECD Trade Policy Papers*, No. 177, OECD Publishing, Paris, *http://dx.doi.org/10.1787/5js7n8wbtk9r*.

Nordstrøm, H. (2017), "Korea 3.0: Unleashing the services economy", *OECD Trade Policy Papers*, OECD Publishing, Paris, forthcoming.

Miroudot, S. and K. Pertel (2015), "Water in the GATS: Methodology and results", *OECD Trade Policy Papers*, No. 185, OECD Publishing, Paris, *http://dx.doi.org/10.1787/5jrs6k35nnf1-en*.

OECD (2015a), *OECD digital economy outlook 2015*, OECD Publishing, Paris, *http://dx.doi.org/10.1787/9789264232440-en*.

OECD (2015b), *Entrepreneurship at a glance*, OECD Publishing Paris, *http://dx.doi.org/10.1787/entrepreneur_aag-2015-en*.

World Bank (2016), "World Bank Doing Business Indicators 2016", available at: *www.doingbusiness.org/data/exploretopics/dealing-with-construction-permits*.

World Economic Forum (2016), "The global competitiveness report 2015-2016", available at: *www3.weforum.org/docs/gcr/2015-2016/Global_Competitiveness_Report_2015-2016.pdf*.

Chapter 3

The benefits of open services markets

Chapter 3 presents evidence that services trade impediments severely affect trade, which has wide-ranging consequences for other areas of economic performance. It reviews the findings of recent OECD analysis of the effect of restrictions on services sectors themselves, as well as in downstream industries that use services as intermediate inputs. The chapter also presents initial insights from on-going OECD analysis to develop trade cost equivalents for services barriers. Finally, it reports the preliminary findings of work estimating the value of commitments made in international trade agreements, particularly in terms of enhancing transparency and predictability in trade and investment.

Services generate more than two-thirds of global GDP, attract over three quarters of foreign direct investment (FDI) in advanced economies, employ most workers and create most new jobs globally. While the shift towards a service economy happens at earlier and earlier stages of development, trade policy has not always followed suit and impediments to global services trade remain more pervasive than in the manufacturing sector. Services trade restrictions create losses for firms that have a tougher time penetrating foreign markets, for household and business customers that are shut out from access to more diversified services at the best price, and for workers that lose the opportunities that would come from more exports and FDI. Conversely, integration in global networks as an exporter or as an FDI recipient can bring about streams of local value creation, innovation and quality jobs that are forgone every time restrictive policies deter a firm from expanding abroad.

Trade in services involves different business models through which firms best serve the needs of their overseas customers. A services provider can directly export abroad, for instance if it sells software through digital means (*Mode 1*: cross-border trade). Firms can also set up local affiliates when proximity to customers matters, as when a commercial bank opens a network of retail branches in a promising market (*Mode 3*: commercial presence). Service-exporting firms can send professionals abroad on a short-term basis, for example engineers co-designing projects locally with the client or technicians travelling to install and repair equipment (*Mode 4*: movement of natural persons). Lastly, international trade also comprises services provided in the firm's own country to non-residents, primarily in the tourism industry (*Mode 2*: consumption abroad). These distinct business models often complement each other for firms wishing to offer a full suite of services to customers. In so doing, services exporters may have to overcome trade costs induced by the general policy environment as well as by policies that target each mode of supply.

To reap the full benefits of trade openness and regulatory reforms, policy makers need to identify regulatory bottlenecks and assess the trade-promoting or trade-restricting impact of policies in place. There are several dimensions through which regulations can depress trade and broader economic outcomes: being restrictive, inconsistent or unpredictable. The Services Trade Restrictiveness Index's primary intent is to focus on the restrictiveness of trade and investment policies towards foreign services providers. At the same time, it can also be used to assess the costs of complying with different regulatory frameworks in different jurisdictions, as well as those of policy uncertainty arising from the gap between applied policies and international commitments.

A common way of quantifying the effects of trade policies is to convert indicators such as the STRI into *ad valorem* trade cost equivalents, or in other words to estimate how high a tariff-like instrument would need to be in order to produce a similar trade-depressing effect. *Ad valorem* equivalents are expressed as a percentage of the value of services provided abroad and provide an easy way to understand quantification of restrictiveness. It should, however, be kept in mind that these estimates necessarily provide a simplified view of a complex and highly diverse range of regulations, creating costs that may not always be proportional to the amount traded and that may not fall equally on all exporters and investors.

Empirical analysis[1] reveals that the costs of services trade and investment barriers are high, largely exceeding the average tariff on traded goods, and that these costs apply to all modes of supplying services abroad. For instance, the average level of restrictions in force in the telecommunications sector amounts to trade costs of up to 150% on cross-border exports and 73% on foreign affiliate sales for highly customised services.

Those trade costs arise both from policies that explicitly target foreign suppliers, and more generally from domestic regulation falling short of best practice in the area of competition and rule-making. Further opening up of services markets through negotiations remains important for reducing trade costs, but attention should also be paid to reviewing sectoral regulations, as well as the efficiency of administrative and licensing procedures, to ensure they do not place an undue burden on new competitors.

Differences in how countries regulate the provision of the same service create additional costs for exporters that need to adapt to new sets of rules in each new market. Regulatory co-operation has taken centre stage in trade and investment negotiations, but regulatory convergence in practice remains scant. When markets are relatively open, trade costs imposed by the average degree of regulatory differences range from 20% to 80%. However, lifting existing restrictions where they are still high should come first. Harmonising the rules of the game brings by far the largest gains when the countries undertaking regulatory co-operation have already brought down their trade barriers.

As services trade restrictions are eased and regulatory co-operation makes tangible progress, small and medium-sized enterprises (SMEs) are the first to gain. The costs of dealing with regulatory hurdles and complying with diverging regulations in every new market fall more heavily on smaller exporters. Often, SMEs find that identifying the regulatory requirements of each country, adapting production methods and documenting compliance is beyond their capacity and give up seeking new customers in new markets. Reducing the costs of market entry would help improve the inclusiveness of services trade by allowing more SMEs to take up global opportunities.

With a strong potential for improving business dynamism, reviving competition and promoting FDI attractiveness, open markets and pro-competitive reforms in services can be an engine for productivity growth and competitiveness throughout the economy. In some segments of the transport and logistics chain, the trade restrictions in place raise prices by an average of about 20% for business users of services inputs, which ultimately falls on consumers. More intense competitive pressure could go a long way to secure better access to world-class services at attractive prices, thereby helping manufacturing firms compete on price and quality.

This chapter first presents the overall trade costs induced by the STRI for the different modes of supply. In all instances, the effects presented below should be understood as expected long-run outcomes of services trade liberalisation after economic actors adjust to the new policy environment, rather than as immediate responses.[2] It then delves into the distribution of these costs among firms of different size, maturity and activities, and the overall benefits of better services regulation for the broader economy. Lastly, the main policy implications are outlined.

The costs of services trade restrictions

It is a well-established fact that international trade is more costly than domestic sales. These costs involve monetary factors, such as shipping, insurance and tariffs. Non-monetary factors, such as transport time or the challenge of enforcing contracts in a foreign jurisdiction, are also quantifiable. Information on the size of trade costs from policy barriers is particularly important for well-informed policy decisions. Services regulation can make trade more costly in a variety of ways, two of which are explored in this section. Most evidently, it can be expected that more stringent services trade restrictions in a country represent higher trade costs. In addition, there is evidence that bilateral trade costs also arise from the heterogeneity of regulation between importing and exporting countries. A third source of trade costs is uncertainty due to the fact that countries often apply policies that are more liberal than their commitments under international agreements, but which therefore cannot be counted on to prevail in the future.

Services trade barriers create large costs for exporters

Empirical analysis shows that the cost of cross-border trade in services resulting from protectionist and anti-competitive regulation is an order of magnitude larger than remaining tariffs for trade in goods. The average STRI[3] in each sector represents trade costs that lie between 142% and 1800% for courier services, between 115% and 1191% for commercial banking, between 31% and 149% for telecommunication services and between 32% and 154% for construction services.[4] Figure 3.1 shows the patterns of trade costs over a larger range of restrictiveness.

Figure 3.1. *Ad valorem* trade cost equivalents for cross-border exports

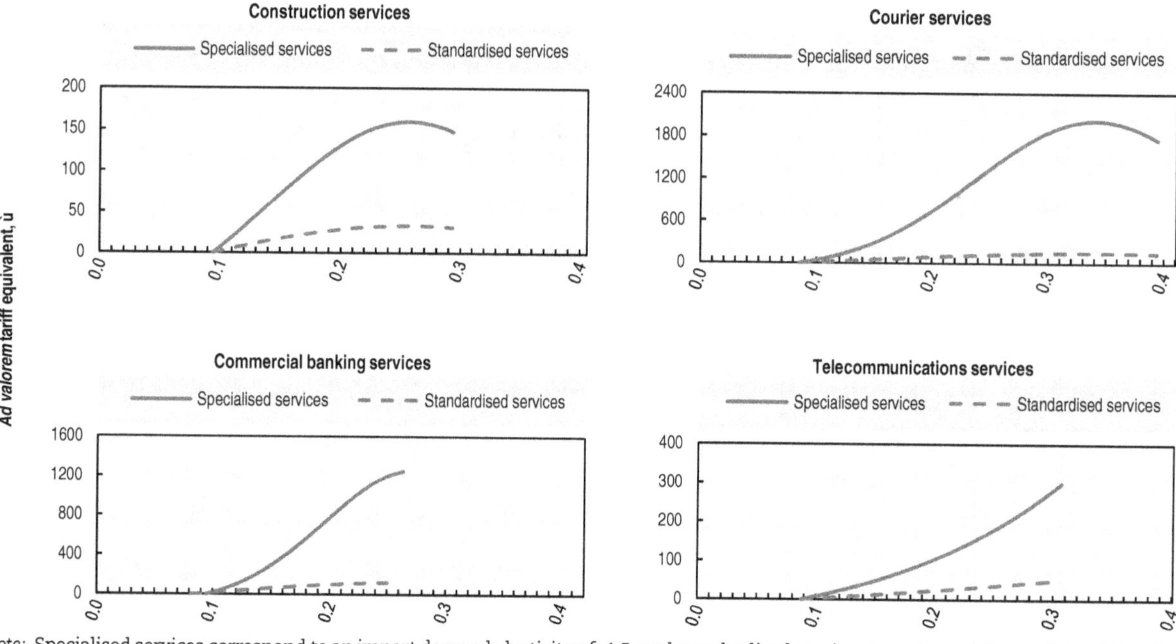

Note: Specialised services correspond to an import demand elasticity of -1.5, and standardised services to an import demand elasticity of -5.
Source: OECD calculations; see Benz (2017).

Sales of foreign affiliates seem to be slightly less affected by restrictive services regulation in *ad valorem* terms.[5] However, since foreign affiliates usually sell larger volumes in a foreign market than the average cross-border exporter, total trade costs may be comparable across the two strategies. In transport services, the average level of services trade restrictiveness generates costs of commercial establishment that correspond to a mark-up between 51% and 292% on all sales of foreign affiliates (Figure 3.2). For foreign affiliates in the computer services sector, the average STRI represents trade barriers that raise the cost of supplying services by an amount equivalent to a tariff of 31% for standard services, and of 147% for specialised services. For telecommunication services, these figures are 18% and 73%, respectively. In the distribution sector, which accounts for a major share of trade via affiliate sales in most countries, trade costs are still far from negligible. On average, trade restrictions in that sector generate trade costs equivalent to a tariff of 10% (standard services) and 37% (specialised services).[6]

Figure 3.2. **Foreign affiliate sales trade cost**

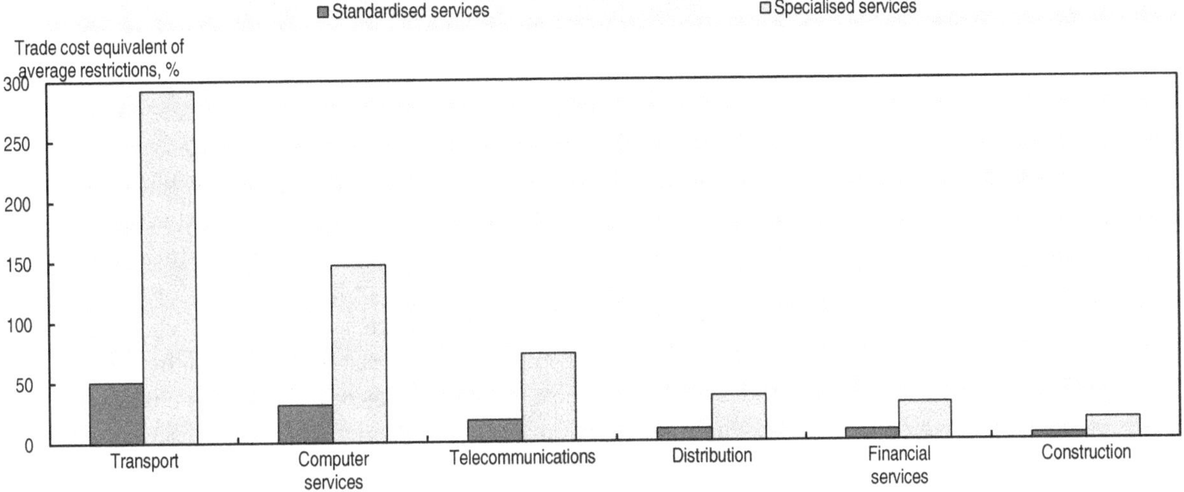

Note: Specialised services correspond to an import demand elasticity of -1.5, and standardised services to an import demand elasticity of -5.
Source: OECD calculations; see Rouzet et al. (2017).

Trade cost equivalents are typically lower where services are relatively standardised. One example is courier services for standard letters for which quality differences in the provision of the service are small. For such services, consumers react strongly to even small changes in price by shifting demand towards cheaper suppliers. Conversely, suppliers of specialised services have more market power and can raise prices as alternatives are not easily found. This is often because they provide a quality that cannot be matched by competitors or they tailor the services to match the needs of each customer. Evidence suggests that banking and professional services are relatively more specialised while distribution is a relatively standardised sector. This means that trade costs for banking services are more likely to be at the upper end of the indicated range while they tend towards the middle of that range for most other services categories and they are at the lower end for distribution services.

Typically these trade costs do not increase linearly with the level of services trade restrictions. For cross-border trade there is some evidence that initial restrictions in relatively liberal environments tend to be more costly than additional restrictions introduced in more restrictive regimes. A potential explanation for this pattern is that above a certain threshold, trade costs might already be prohibitively high for exporting firms. Alternatively, higher degrees of restrictiveness may result in a situation in which a regulatory tightening does not further restrict the company's business model because only a limited range of functions is still supplied to the foreign market.

Services are often supplied via a combination of different modes

At first glance, exporting or setting up a local affiliate are alternative means of reaching consumers abroad. Firms may choose between these modes of delivery by weighing the additional cost of a local establishment and the risk of a less agile model against the benefits of proximity to local consumers. However, there is some evidence that the modes of supply complement each other. In addition, cross-border exports as well as foreign affiliate sales seem to depend on the free movement of natural persons. Potential explanations are that large projects require a combination of different modes or that different segments of the customer base are served best through different channels. For example, in the construction sector, barriers to commercial presence (Mode 3) account for the lion's share of the costs affecting cross-border exports in the sector. Barriers to Mode 3 also contribute to cross-border trade costs in courier services and telecommunication services.

Restrictions behind the border represent important barriers to cross-border trade and to affiliate sales. Especially in the telecommunications and maritime transport services sectors, cross-border exports are affected by weak enforcement of competition such as shipping agreements being exempt from competition law, inadequate regulation of dominant telecommunications providers, or lack of transparency with respect to procedures and regulation. Similarly, most important barriers to sales of foreign affiliates seem to arise behind the border, as summarised in Figure 3.3 by restrictions to "All Modes". While weak pro-competitive regulation or a heavy regulatory burden are non-discriminatory in the sense that both domestic suppliers and their foreign competitors are affected, foreign suppliers are often more severely hampered due to their unfamiliarity with regulation and their being required to cope with different types of restrictions in different countries. This result highlights the importance of extending best-practice regulation and liberalisation beyond market access and national treatment restrictions. In fact, discriminatory barriers seem to be

Figure 3.3. **Breakdown of foreign affiliate sales trade cost**

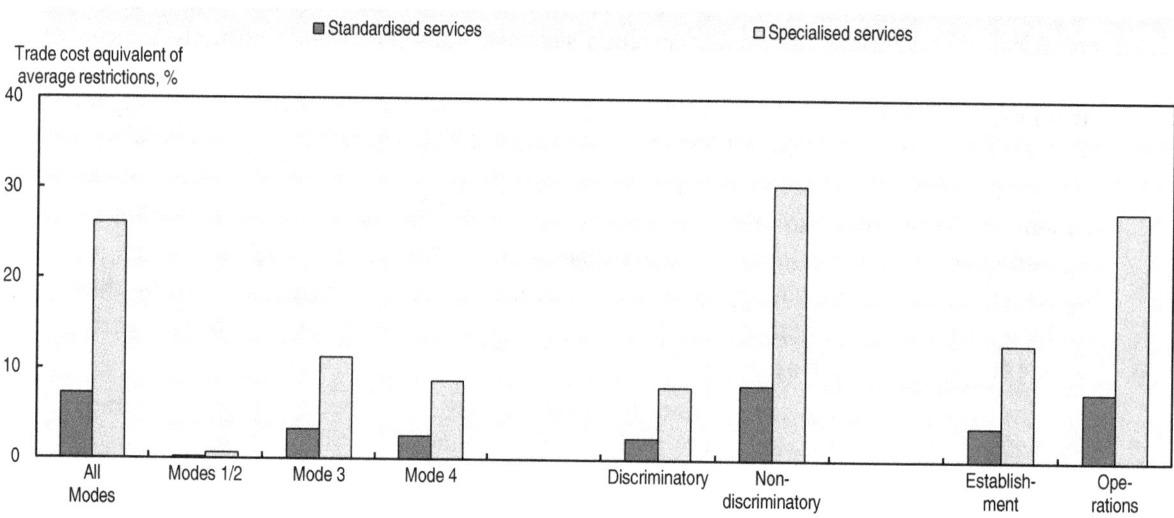

Note: Specialised services correspond to an import demand elasticity of -1.5, and standardised services to an import demand elasticity of -5.
Source: OECD calculations; see Rouzet et al. (2017).

relatively less important for the decision to establish a commercial presence in a foreign market than the overall business environment.

Commercial presence abroad also seems to rely heavily on the accompanying movement of people from headquarters to the affiliate, as shown by the contribution of barriers to Mode 4 to the costs of selling abroad through affiliates (Figure 3.3). Barriers to Mode 4 also explain a major share of trade costs for cross-border trade in courier services and commercial banking services, even though their contribution to the STRI score is relatively small in most countries. This indicates that many firms with a commercial presence abroad actually export via a combination of different modes and that affiliates may be more successful where they are also able to trade services back and forth with their headquarters. Policy should therefore aim towards liberalisation jointly in the areas of trade and investment in order not to distort the choices of exporters and to maximise the resulting benefits.

The benefits of liberalisation depend on an industry's predominant organisational model

The business models for value creation in services are diverse and are not always organised in the form of a "value chain".[7] In fact, the most prevalent organisational model is the "value shop", accounting for 50% of employment in major economies, in which value is created by experts and professionals using tailored solutions to solve specific customer problems. Another model is the "value network", which creates value by linking customers with different needs, as in banking and insurance services; networks of physical infrastructure and "virtual platforms" like Uber or Airbnb are types of value networks.

Specific trade policy measures do not necessarily affect all organisational models. Services in value chains are often bundled with goods, making them sensitive to tariffs and non-tariff barriers to trade in goods, custom procedures or the lack of efficient infrastructure at ports and airports. By contrast, barriers to the movement of people are most relevant for value shops, which are largely traded via Mode 4 and rely on the access to skills and the access to customers.

Barriers to competition typically affect physical value networks where market imperfections need to be addressed through pro-competitive regulations within the country. A requirement of commercial presence is often the main restriction for virtual networks. It may arise in the form of restrictions to data flows, such as requirements of data localisation, which restricts trade even when designed to protect consumer rights.

Regulatory co-operation can reduce trade costs

Above and beyond the costs of dealing with restrictive policies, merely having to comply with regulations in target markets that differ notably from those of the home country is also costly for exporters. The heterogeneity of services regulation across countries is substantial and appears to be significantly receding in only a minority of sectors. For relatively liberalised countries with a very low STRI score of 0.1, the average degree of regulatory heterogeneity between two countries can account for *ad valorem* costs of cross-border trade between 20% and 80%, on average over all sectors (Figure 3.4). In more restrictive countries with an STRI score of 0.25 such heterogeneity still represents trade costs of between 12% and 45%.[8] In other words, as countries open up their markets, regulatory differences become more costly. This effect does not outweigh the benefits of liberalisation, but it may slightly reduce them. The results show that regulatory co-operation can substantially stimulate services trade and that such cooperation becomes even more crucial when a sector has already reached an advanced stage of liberalisation.

Figure 3.4. **The cost of regulatory heterogeneity for cross-border exports**

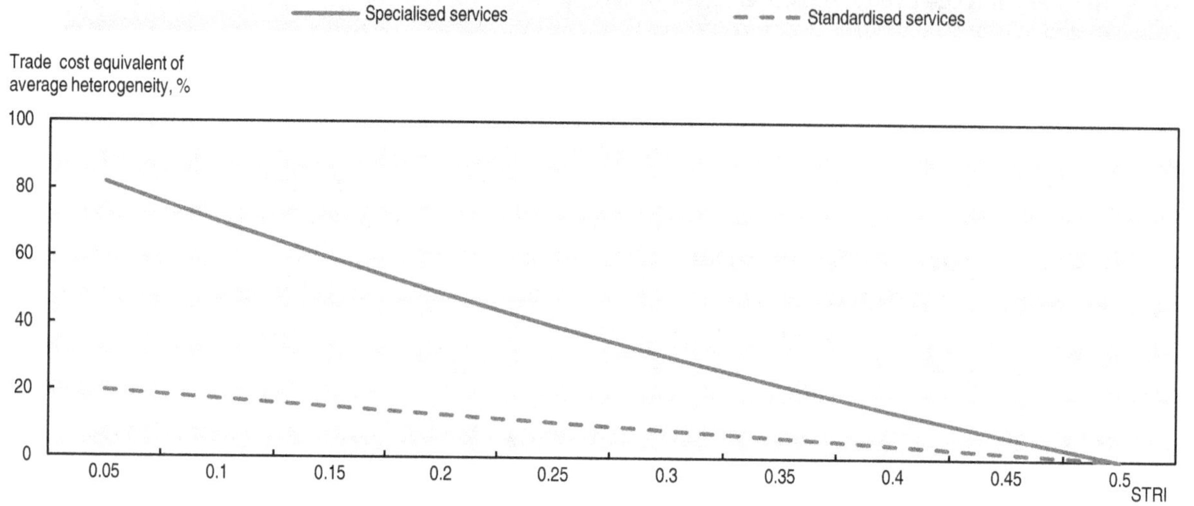

Note: Specialised services correspond to an import demand elasticity of -1.5, and standardised services to an import demand elasticity of -5. Average regulatory heterogeneity among the 44 countries in the STRI database is 0.28. Regression lines are based on a pooled sample of cross-border exports between countries in the STRI database.
Source: OECD calculations; see Nordås (2016).

A predictable regulatory environment supports trade in services

While the heterogeneity in regulations creates costs for exporters, another source of potential costs comes from the unpredictability of the trade regime and the risk of policy reversals. Both exports and establishment abroad involve costs that are often sunk in the sense that once incurred, they cannot be recovered when a change in regulation no longer makes the foreign market profitable. Services providers are therefore more likely to engage in trade when they receive some guarantee that the regulatory regime will not become more restrictive in the future. This is precisely the role assigned to trade agreements covering services trade. These agreements include legal bindings that in some cases offer better market access to foreign providers, but that also have value when they simply bind the existing regime by offering a more predictable regulatory environment.

This positive impact of services trade agreements has been discussed for a long time in the trade literature following the entry into force of the General Agreement on Trade in Services (GATS) and the rapid increase in regional trade agreements (RTAs) covering services. However, it is only with the development of STRI indices providing a detailed account of all regulatory measures affecting trade in services that it has become possible to measure to what extent trade agreements bind the existing regime. Calculations done at the OECD have shown that there is some heterogeneity across countries and sectors (Box 3.1).

Binding the existing regime has a direct impact on the volume of bilateral trade, confirming that a predictable regulatory environment supports trade. By combining the information on the water in the GATS (Box 3.1) with further analysis of commitments made in RTAs, one can estimate the implied response of trade to the reduction in the uncertainty of the trade regime. For most services sectors in the STRI database, positive and significant effects are found. They are often in the same range as the ones observed for an actual reduction in the level of trade restrictiveness (i.e. a decrease in STRI indices).

Box 3.1. **To what extent are trade agreements binding in current services trade regimes?**

Services trade agreements, such as the GATS, include market access and national treatment commitments that provide some guarantee to services exporters that the regime they face will not become more restrictive in the future than the level specified in the agreement. The difference between the bound level of restrictiveness permitted by the agreement and the actual trade regime is called the "water". The higher the level of this water, the less predictable the trade regime is for potential exporters since countries can arbitrarily raise barriers within this interval without breaching their international agreements .

Figure 3.5 illustrates the heterogeneity across sectors in the level of the "water" in GATS commitments. For sectors like telecoms, distribution, computer services or construction, a predictable trade environment is offered to exporters at the multilateral level with market access and national treatment commitments being very close to the existing applied regime. For other sectors, such as audio-visual or transport services, there is more uncertainty. Regional trade agreements remove some of this uncertainty by going further than the GATS at the bilateral or regional level.

Figure 3.5. **Average water in the GATS for selected STRI sectors**

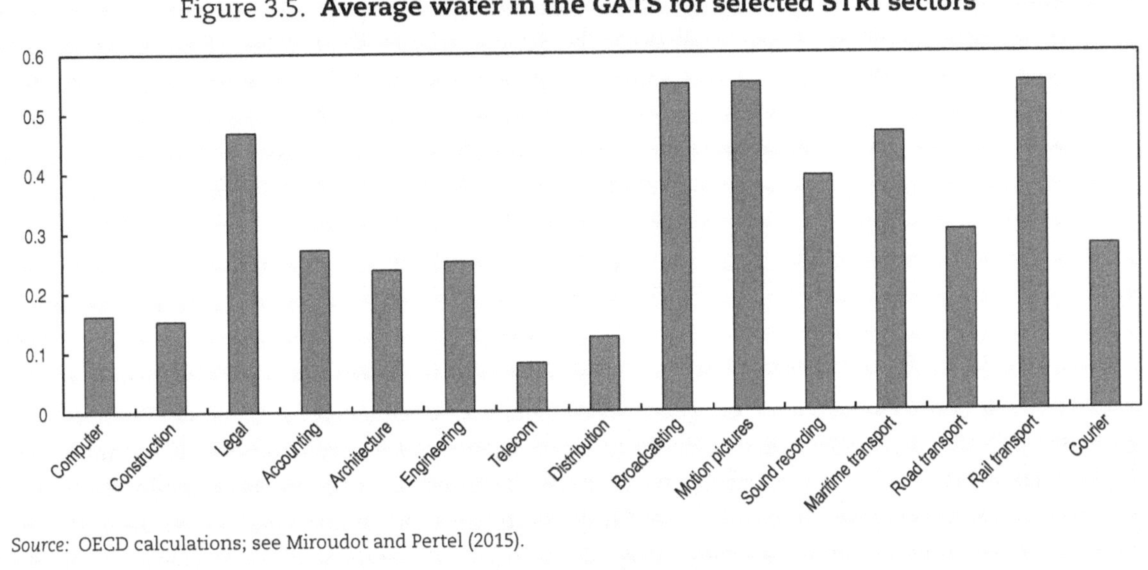

Source: OECD calculations; see Miroudot and Pertel (2015).

These results suggest that even when they do not actually remove trade barriers, services trade agreements still play a positive role through their legal bindings and the reduction in the uncertainty for services exporters.

Small countries suffer more from services trade barriers and may gain more from liberalisation

Country specificities play a role in how laws and regulations came to be and how the policy environment has a bearing on economic and social outcomes. Because of limitations in data and methodology, individual country-level differences with respect to the cost of a given policy stance cannot be robustly identified. However, a general pattern is that the trade effect of restrictions decreases with market size. In other words, a given element of regulatory liberalisation yields a larger increase of services trade in countries with a smaller GDP than in countries with a higher GDP. This is consistent with the hypothesis that larger internal markets make an economy less dependent on international trade, which also manifests itself in higher ratios of exports and imports to GDP in smaller economies.

So far, all trade costs have been measured in *ad valorem* terms, representing a mark-up over the price that is paid by consumers in the importing country. Such analysis shows that the benefits of services trade liberalisation are not spread equally across countries and sectors. Hence, an in-depth analysis of reform should be conducted in order to gain information on target sectors and policy barriers in order to maximise the economic gains from a services regulation reform agenda. However, while the economic effectiveness of reform is paramount for its success, no less important is the distribution of gains across the economy. The distribution of these gains is imminently linked to the structural composition of trade barriers into variable costs, fixed costs and sunk costs, requiring an analysis that goes beyond the calculation of aggregate *ad valorem* trade cost equivalents. The following section will therefore present more information on the decomposition of trade costs into different structural components and on how the gains of services trade liberalisation are distributed across firms.

A more inclusive globalisation of services?

While the previous section highlighted the aggregate costs of regulatory restrictions, it bears noting that these costs are not equally spread among services traders and investors. As the international community strives to design trade rules for a more inclusive globalisation, a key question is identifying which businesses lose out as a result of existing trade barriers, and in turn which firms would benefit most from further services liberalisation. It emerges that SMEs and new entrants are the hardest hit by policy impediments to trade in services, such that regulatory reform would help diversify export and growth opportunities for some of the most dynamic and job-creating actors of the services economy.

Services liberalisation spurs new entry into export markets by less experienced firms

Services trade barriers not only depress trade in services in aggregate, but also narrow the prospects of pioneer exporters by favouring experienced incumbents over firms that try to penetrate a new market for the first time. Every time a country opens up moderately to services trade so that its STRI falls by 0.1, the probability that a firm with no established trade relationship there start exporting to that country increases by between 2 and 12 percentage points. In contrast, liberalisation does not significantly boost the likelihood that incumbent exporters will remain in the market.

Even when they do manage to enter, the same restrictions are more costly for new entrants than for repeat exporters. For example, in a relatively restrictive market characterised by an STRI score of 0.4, new exporters have to incur costs equivalent to an additional 14 to 53 *ad valorem* percentage points on top of the regulatory costs faced by incumbent exporters (Figure 3.6). As newly created firms are primarily engaged in the service economy and, by definition, start doing business without export experience, co-ordinated services trade liberalisation could therefore emerge as a tool to boost start-up dynamism at the global level.

The penalty for new entrants reflects the importance of initial barriers in the overall burden of restrictive regulations. One can distinguish one-off entry costs, recurrent fixed costs and *ad valorem* variable costs (Box 3.2). Evidence from firm-level data suggests that while policy-induced variable costs are far from trivial, a substantive share of the trade-restricting impact of regulations is accounted for by fixed and sunk costs, which are borne irrespective of how much is actually sold in a foreign market. Such costs come for instance

Figure 3.6. **Additional trade cost of regulatory restrictions for new exporters**
Estimated additional tariff equivalent of the STRI index compared to experienced exporters

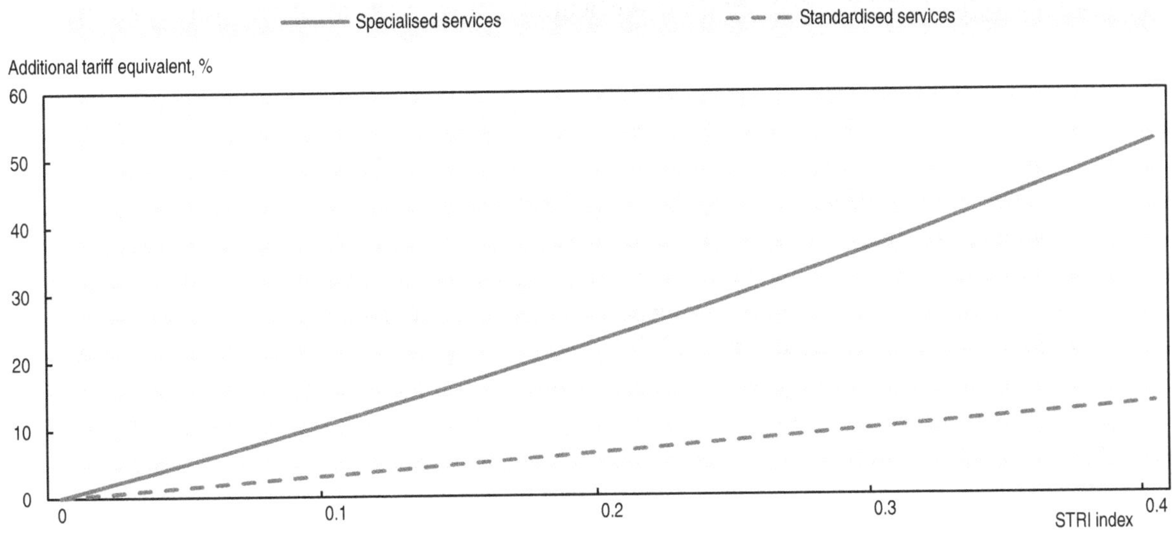

Note: The numbers indicate the additional *ad valorem* tariff equivalent for firms without export experience, where export experience is defined as having exported the same service to the same country in the previous year. Specialised services correspond to an import demand elasticity of -1.5, and standardised services to an import demand elasticity of -5.
Source: OECD calculations; see Rouzet et al. (2017).

Box 3.2. **Entry costs, fixed costs and variable costs**

Trade costs, whether they arise from actionable policies or more structural geographical, historical or preference factors, come in various shapes and forms. A main distinction can be made between variable trade costs and fixed trade costs, with different implications for the extent to which trade restrictions affect the decision to enter a market (called the extensive margin) and the volume of exports conditional on entry (called the intensive margin).

Fixed trade costs may either recur each period or they may take the form of a one-time payment. Entry costs or sunk costs are incurred once and for all the first time a firm penetrates a foreign market. Such costs arise, for instance, from screening procedures for foreign investment, or demanding processes for the recognition of professional qualifications acquired abroad by foreign engineers, accountants or lawyers. They reduce the probability that firms that have not previously sold in a given market will decide to do so, but they have no impact on the probability of remaining in the market for repeat exporters or on the amount actually sold by active exporters.

Another type of fixed trade cost must be paid on a recurring basis, also regardless of how much activity is undertaken in the host country. For instance, burdensome renewal processes for licences to operate in a foreign market, data localisation requirements, or economic-needs tests for key personnel are likely to comprise a strong fixed cost component. High fixed costs discourage both new and repeat exporters from trading in a country altogether, but do not influence the amount exported once a firm has decided to serve a market.

Once a firm has paid all fixed trade costs, the volume of exports is only determined by variable or ad valorem trade costs, proportional to the value of services sold. Discriminatory regulations affecting foreign firms' on-going operations in an overseas market, such as higher taxes on sales or profits generated by foreign suppliers or local sourcing requirements, tend to be of this nature. The effect of variable trade costs is the most similar effect to that of tariffs: they discourage entry into foreign markets and also reduce the amount exported by firms that do sell abroad.

in the form of identifying and understanding the regulatory framework in place, adapting business processes to the requirements of the local regulators, or dealing with the administrative hurdles of acquiring and renewing a license to operate. Their primary effect is to reduce the number of firms that find it worthwhile to do business in a foreign market. Indeed, the number of foreign firms that establish trade relationships with partners in a given country is reduced where this country imposes more severe restrictions in the sector.

SMEs bear the highest cost from restrictive trade policies

Smaller firms often expand internationally by pursuing a niche strategy or providing a suite of customised services to few clients. The digital economy has raised hopes that it would breed countless such opportunities for small and medium enterprises to go global in a borderless world. Yet borders are still highly relevant in services regulation and where high entry and fixed costs mean that scaling up and attaining critical mass rapidly is a precondition for success, SMEs are the most harmed by restrictions. Fixed trade costs are all the more costly to absorb for firms that export modest amounts as those costs cannot be spread over a large volume of foreign sales. Larger firms with deep financial resources and extensive networks of business partners are also better equipped to overcome the compliance cost of exporting in complex regulatory environments, and may have sufficient market power to pass the cost of regulation on to consumers. As a result, smaller would-be exporters are the first to be discouraged from entering more restrictive markets at all, and they realise lower sales in those markets if they do manage to recoup the cost of entry.

In other words, a given level of regulatory restrictions represents larger trade costs for smaller firms. For instance, an average level of service trade restrictiveness corresponding to a score of 0.2 on the STRI is as costly as an additional tariff of up to 14 percentage points on small firms' exports, relative to large firms with turnover of EUR 400 million and over (Figure 3.7a). In a more restrictive environment represented by an STRI index of 0.3, the extra burden on small firms is compounded and is equivalent to an extra tariff of over 20 percentage points for the smallest firms trading customised services.

Setting up and operating an affiliate abroad involves a wider range of sunk and fixed costs, regulatory or otherwise, than trading on an arm's length basis: acquiring or leasing real estate, tying up capital in the new venture, obtaining the necessary approvals and licenses, recruiting local employees and bringing in highly qualified personnel from headquarters, entail procedures and expenses that come before any service is actually rendered in the host market. It therefore comes as no surprise that regulatory restrictions create even more of an obstacle to invest abroad than to export cross-border for firms that do not enjoy the benefits of scale. For instance, the extra burden of an STRI of 0.2, for a medium-sized firm of EUR 5 million in turnover selling specialised services through foreign affiliates is estimated to be equivalent to an additional 19% tariff compared to large firms, whereas the extra equivalent tariff is 9% on cross-border exports of the same services (Figure 3.7b).

In a similar fashion, differences in regulatory approaches dealing with the same policy issue are more of a deterrent for SMEs. Smaller exporters lack the scale that may make it profitable to invest upfront in adapting to unfamiliar sets of rules. More often than not, SMEs also lack the legal and administrative capacity to gather information about the regulatory requirements in new markets, adapt their processes and document compliance where those requirements differ widely from regulation at home.

Figure 3.7. **Additional trade cost of regulatory restrictions for SMEs**

Estimated additional tariff equivalent of an STRI of 0.2 compared to large firms of EUR 400 million or more

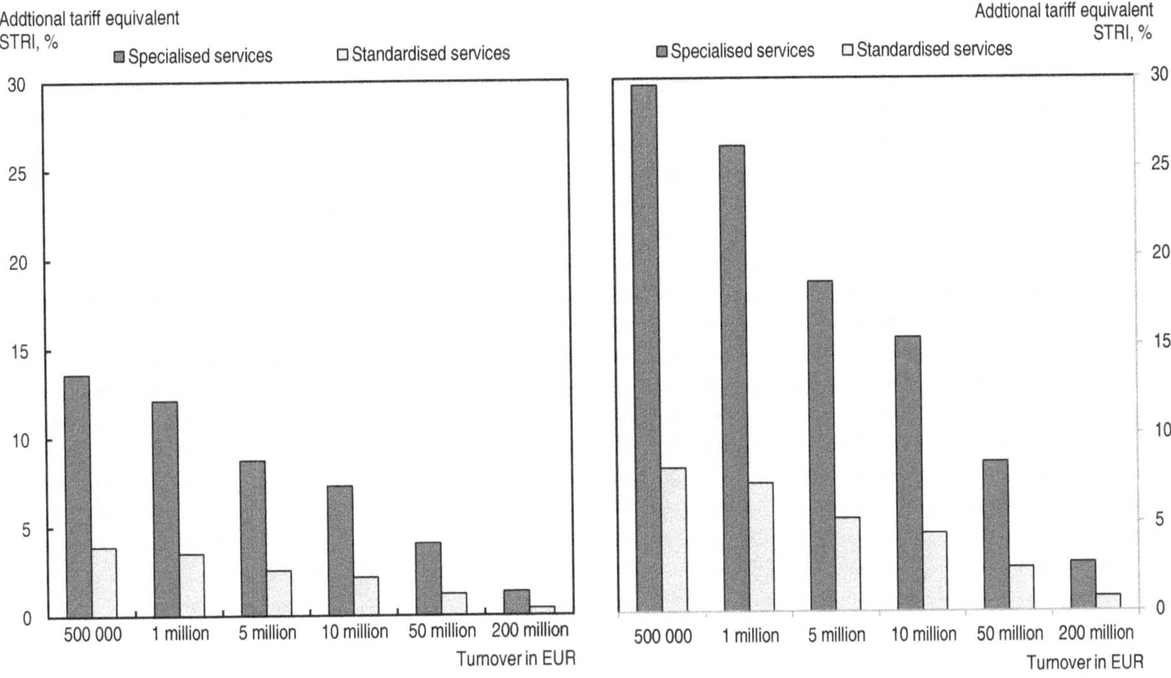

Note: The numbers indicate the *ad valorem* tariff equivalent of an STRI score of 0.2 for small and medium-sized enterprises on top of what is paid by firms of 400 million and more in turnover. Specialised services correspond to an import demand elasticity of -1.5, and standardised services to an import demand elasticity of -5.

Source: OECD calculations; see Rouzet et al. (2017).

Firms with multiple ties to the host market are better able to deal with regulatory hurdles

Which other factors, apart from size and experience, increase firms' immunity to the effects of restrictive policies in their target markets? Some firms do not only aim to expand their customer base abroad, but appear to have an overarching reason to sell services in a specific country rather than seeking more favourable conditions elsewhere; these firms are less sensitive to the services trade policies they encounter. Two such motives stand out: providing services to the exporter's foreign headquarters or as complement to its parent's local activity, and adding value to manufacturing exports though services activities.

First, firms that are subsidiaries of a foreign corporate group have a particular advantage when dealing with restrictive regulations in the country of their parent. When a country has an STRI score of 0.4, the *ad valorem* equivalent of the cost of services trade restrictions is between 4 and 14 percentage points lower for firms that are subsidiaries of a parent firm in that country than for firms with no ownership ties to the target market (Figure 3.8a). This suggests that affiliates of foreign firms benefit from their parent company's knowledge of how to navigate complex requirements in the headquarter country. Moreover, exports back to the home country include services provided to the parent firm. Intra-firm transactions are likely to be driven by an established division of tasks within the firm and less sensitive to regulatory hurdles than arm's length dealings.

Second, services exported jointly with goods are even less sensitive to policy conditions in the destination market. Firms exporting both goods and services to the same country

Figure 3.8. **Estimated discount on the tariff equivalent of the STRI index for specific firms**

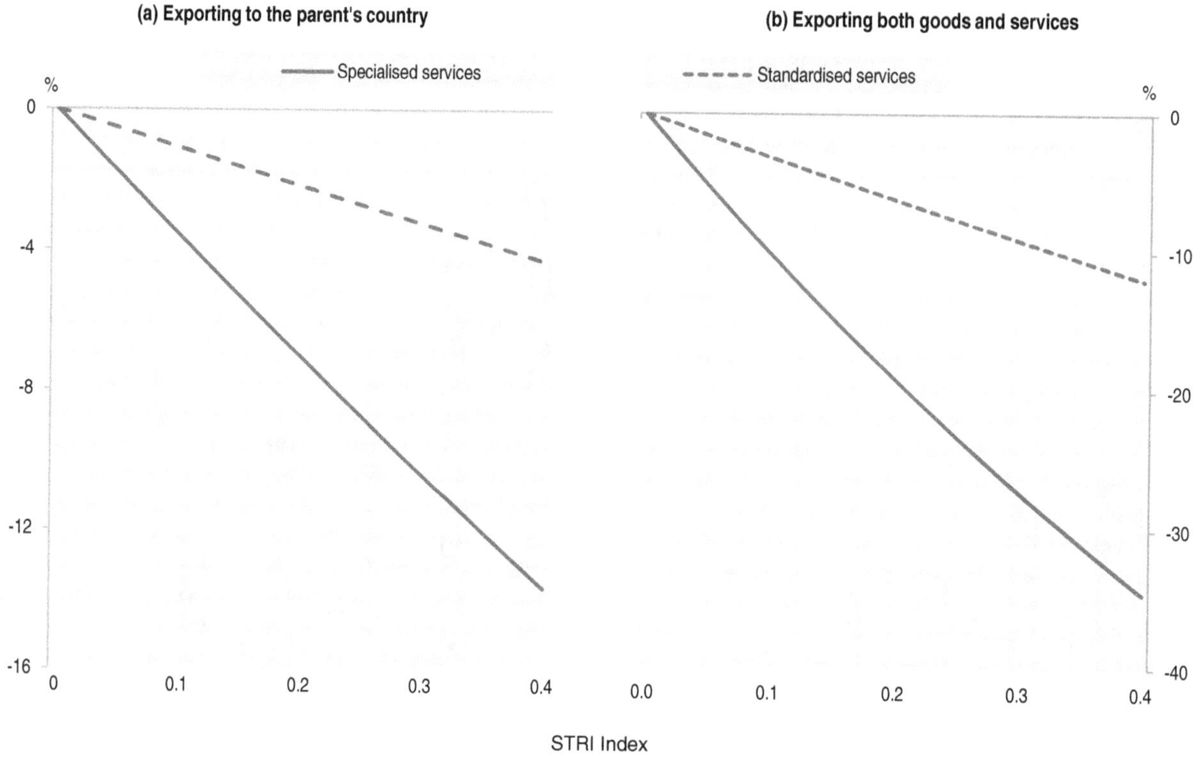

Note: The numbers indicate the amount by which the *ad valorem* tariff equivalent of the STRI is reduced for firms that have headquarters or ultimate owners in the destination markets, compared to firms with no ownership links in the country (left); and for firms also exporting goods to the same country, compared to pure services exporters (right). Specialised services correspond to an import demand elasticity of -1.5, and standardised services to an import demand elasticity of -5.
Source: OECD calculations; see Rouzet et al. (2017).

tend to be present in more restrictive destinations than firms selling services alone. In other words, goods exporters perceive a restrictive policy regime to be less costly for their services packages than exclusive services exporters. For a relatively high STRI score of 0.4, the *ad valorem* tariff equivalent of this discount can be as high as 35 percentage points for customised services (Figure 3.8b). This is probably because, when offering a joint supply of services, goods exporters add value to their manufactured product exports, a phenomenon often referred to as bundling of goods and services (Box 3.3). Where the primary driver of a firm's services exports is demand for exports of its physical products, complying with costly services regulations may be viewed as a necessary means for reaping the gains from manufacturing sales, rather than a prohibitive factor.

Box 3.3. **How do manufacturing firms participate in services trade?**

Evolving models of how firms do business and create value mean that the distinction between goods and services trade has become increasingly blurred. Manufacturing firms both import and export a range of services. Services trade can be driven by manufacturing activities through several channels:

Services inputs imported in market-based transactions. Many services procured from external suppliers are essential inputs in local and global value chains. They enable firms to manage operations seamlessly across facilities and production stages (e.g. transport, logistics, communications, financing, outsourced back-office functions), add value to the products and improve processes (e.g. technical testing, engineering, design

---

Box 3.3. **How do manufacturing firms participate in services trade?** (cont.)

when not conducted in-house). The Trade in Value-Added database has revealed that such services account for about a third of value-added in global manufacturing exports, 40% of which are services imported directly or indirectly by the manufacturers (OECD-WTO, 2017).

Services inputs provided within a corporate group. Some key services are provided in-house, either by the headquarters to affiliates or by a firm's local and offshore subsidiaries to headquarters. Examples are R&D centres, marketing and sales teams, legal counsel, internal audit or human resources. For instance, over 80% of US imports of R&D, business and management consulting and IT services are purchased from within the importer's corporate group, while telecommunication and engineering inputs tend to be outsourced (Figure 3.9).

Figure 3.9. **US services imports by affiliation, 2015**

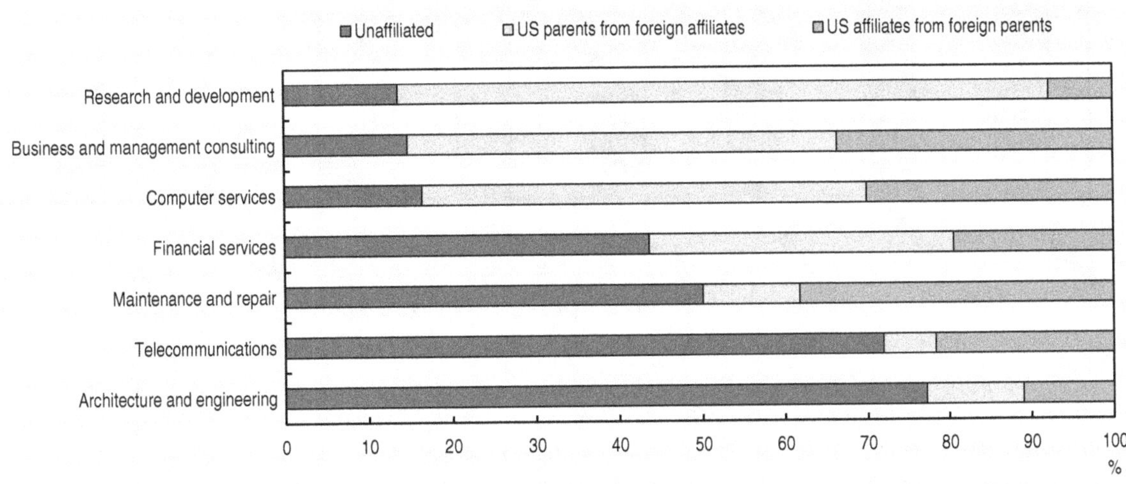

Source: OECD calculations based on data from the US Bureau of Economic Analysis.

Services sold jointly with goods. Firms increasingly offer integrated solutions to their clients, comprising bundles of goods and complementary services. Car manufacturers may operate car dealerships themselves and provide credit and leasing to their customers; high-tech manufacturers sell embedded software, feature customisation, after-sales repair and maintenance services packaged with physical goods. In Finland, where high-tech equipment and electronics dominate industrial exports, manufacturers realised more than four-fifths of total export sales in computer services and a quarter in architecture and engineering services between 2008 and 2014. In Belgium, more than half of exports of architecture, engineering and telecommunications services in 2014 accompanied sales of goods by the same firm to the same country, as did a quarter of computer services sold abroad (Figure 3.10).

Box 3.3. **How do manufacturing firms participate in services trade?** *(cont.)*

Figure 3.10. **Share of bundled and non-bundled services exports in Belgium, 2014**

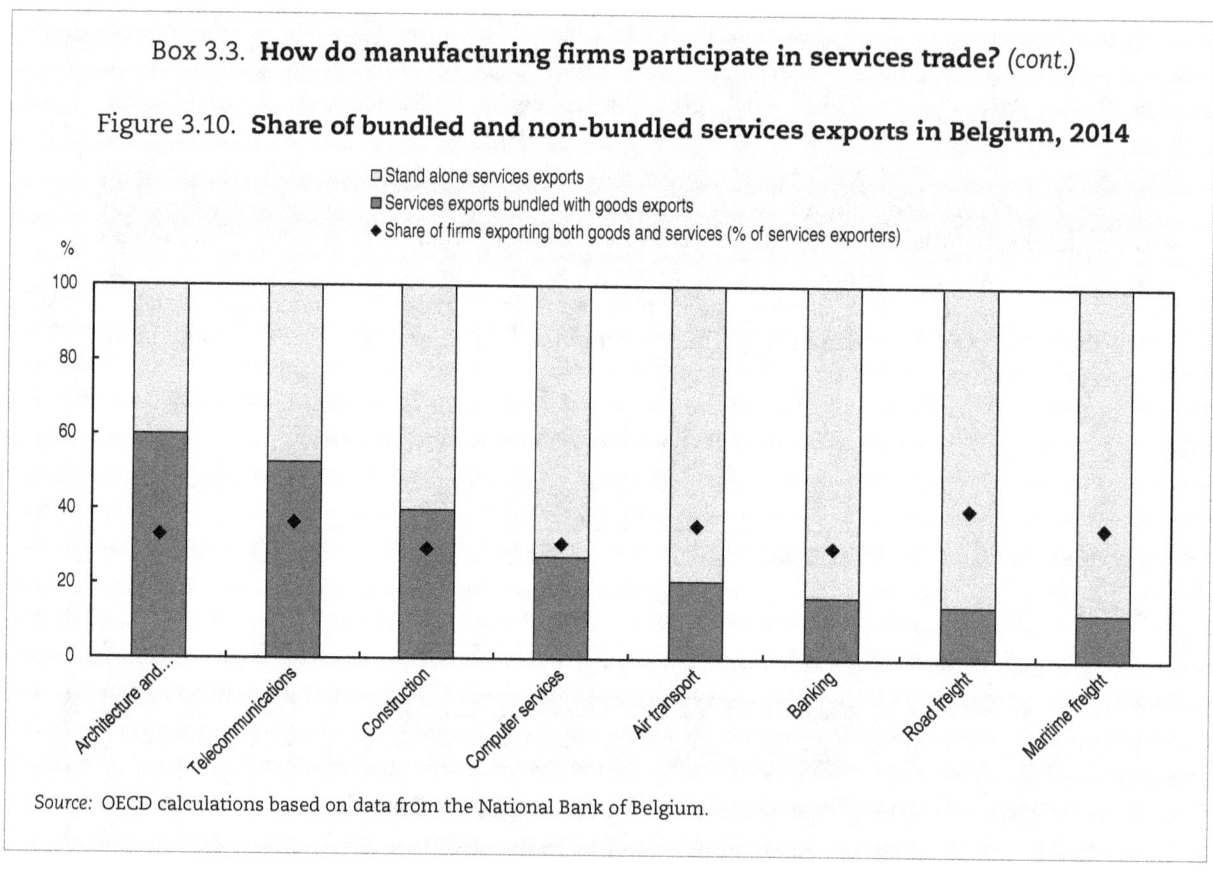

Source: OECD calculations based on data from the National Bank of Belgium.

Services liberalisation

Evidence from the previous sections makes a clear case that impediments to trade and investment weigh on foreign firms' decision to enter new markets via cross-border trade and/or the establishment of an affiliate. Beyond trade itself, inadequate regulation on market entry, competition rules or administrative procedures place a heavy burden on services firms and their customers, impairing overall business dynamism and competitiveness.

Consumers and firms pay the cost of trade restrictions

As well as those restrictions that specifically target foreign firms, it is clear that the role of domestic regulation related to barriers to competition and lack of regulatory transparency should also be examined. When competitive pressures are weakened, incumbent firms tend to consolidate and expand their market power, reducing the chance for disruptive innovation by new players. Restrictive domestic regulation creates a policy environment that discourages new entrants, whether they be potential domestic businesses or foreign competitors. For this reason, the cost of weak competition policy is also covered in the analysis of trade restrictiveness.

The final cost of a policy environment that reduces competition from new entrants, whether domestic or foreign, is ultimately borne by consumers and downstream business customers, which pay higher prices and enjoy less choice than they would in more competitive markets. The resulting price premium for domestic users of services can be quantified as a sales tax equivalent on their purchases.[9] On average across 42 countries, estimates of this tax equivalent range from about 3% in road freight transport to almost

40% in broadcasting, with considerable variation across countries in all sectors (Figure 3.11, Panel A). In some segments of transport and logistics, as well as in construction, restrictive regulations raise the price of services by about 20% on average, and in some countries by almost 80%, imposing substantial additional costs on manufacturing enterprises and eventually on final customers.

Figure 3.11. **Average estimated tax-equivalent of services trade restrictions, by sector**

Panel A. Dispersion over 42 countries of the tax-equivalent estimates

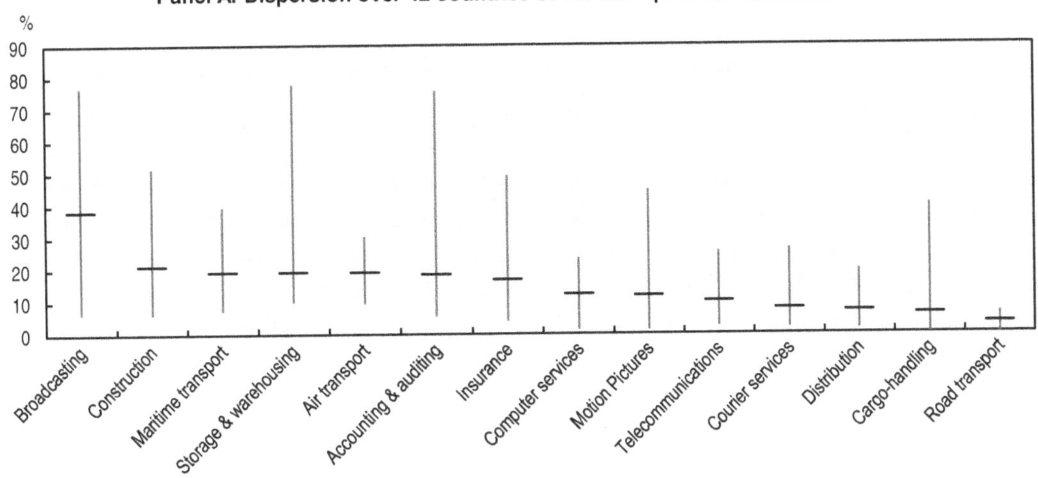

Panel B. Discriminatory and non-discriminatory regulation

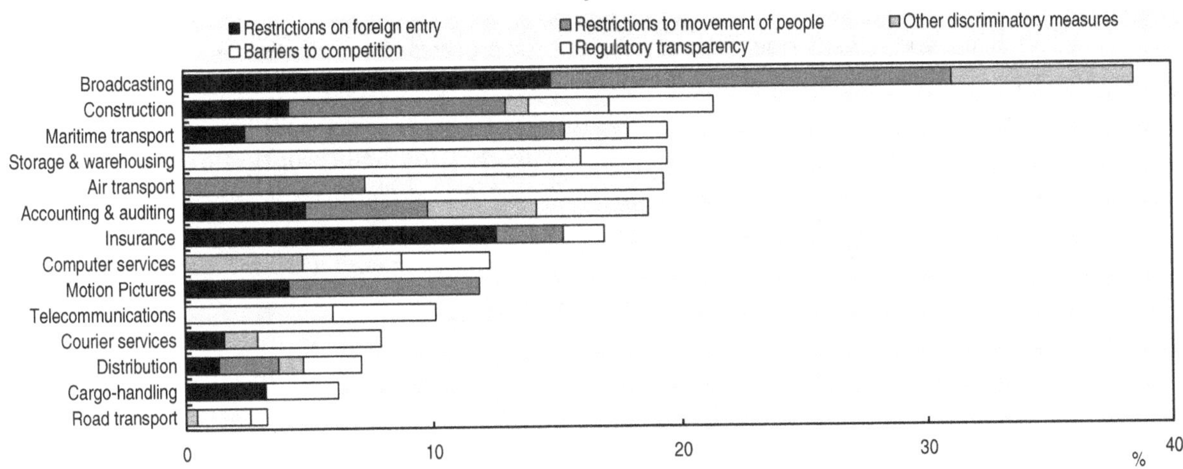

Note: The estimates are simple averages of the tax equivalents observed in 42 countries. Restrictions to foreign entry, to movement of people and other discriminatory measures mostly reflect discriminatory policies, while barriers to competition and lack of regulatory transparency are mainly associated with domestic regulation.
Source: OECD calculations based on the BvD Orbis and STRI databases; see Rouzet and Spinelli (2016).

Inadequacy or lack of enforcement of competition law and opaque rule-making (together with lengthy or costly customs procedures) could be among the main factors explaining high costs of services in telecommunications, transport and logistics, where such impediments allow firms to charge between 10% and 20% more than they would have been able to in more competitive markets (Figure 3.11, Panel B).

While behind-the-border regulation applies equally to domestic and foreign companies established in a given market, it therefore stands out for being just as relevant as discriminatory measures listed in trade and investment negotiations, since ultimately it contributes to raising the cost of services across the board. It follows that substantial pro-competitive gains could be reaped from trade and investment liberalisation, but also from policy reforms targeting inefficient domestic regulation in services markets.

Furthermore, evidence discussed in the previous section has shown that restrictions to services trade introduce substantial entry costs favouring experienced incumbents over exporters venturing into new markets for the first time. Further openness of services trade would thus not only bring overall gains from more intense competitive pressure, but also encourage the entry of young and small firms that start exporting only when market conditions are more favourable, thereby creating a more dynamic and diversified economy.

Efficient intermediate services help manufacturing businesses compete

Intermediate services inputs provide essential links in value chains, from product development to production, marketing and sales. They move parts and components to the assembly line and final products to end-users; they design, engineer and innovate; they monitor demand and consumer tastes, and transmit such information to the product developers; they provide funding and insurance; and they facilitate compliance with laws and regulations in all the markets where the product is sold. Depending on the position in the value chain, intermediate services reduce costs, upgrade quality and match suppliers and customers around the world. Where services regulations depart from best practice, the cost surcharge highlighted above hampers manufacturers competing for market shares abroad: they are less competitive on price and quality, export lower volumes, and are less diversified across markets and products.

A rich and cost-effective services supplier base is a driver of comparative advantage in industries that are intensive users of intermediate services, which are often high-end manufacturing sectors. Taking into account in-house service functions as well as outsourced services used by manufacturing firms, the total contribution of services activities to the value of manufacturing exports ranges across countries between 40% and 60% (Figure 3.12). While offshored services are the most impeded by trade restrictions, the cost and quality of services provided in-house or procured on the domestic market are also likely to be affected by the prevailing competitive conditions.

Figure 3.12. In-house, outsourced and offshored service value-added in manufacturing exports, 2011

As a % of gross exports

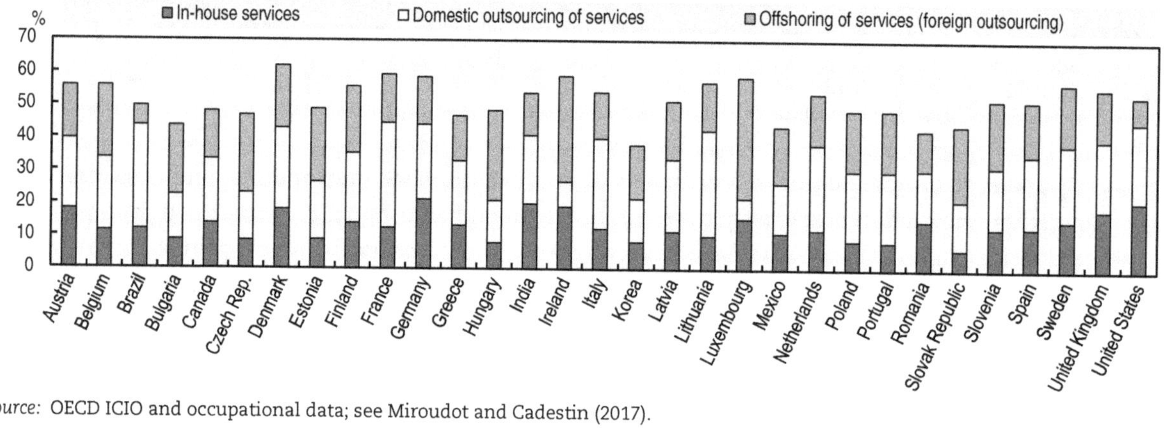

Source: OECD ICIO and occupational data; see Miroudot and Cadestin (2017).

Freight transport directly underpins global trade in components and final goods. It should, therefore, be no surprise that countries with higher restrictions on air, maritime or road transport and courier services are less successful exporters of manufactured goods, particularly in time-sensitive products where speedy and reliable delivery can make or break a sale. Not only do restrictive transport conditions at home translate into lower export volumes, but they also limit the ability of manufacturing industries to reach a large number of foreign markets and to offer a diversified set of products. Figure 3.13 shows that restrictions on road freight (relative to other transport modes) most strongly inhibit exports of various key industries (automotive, electrical equipment and chemicals) (Figure 3.13).

Figure 3.13. Estimated impact of halving the distance to best-practice STRI on manufacturing exports by sector, average of 44 countries, 2014

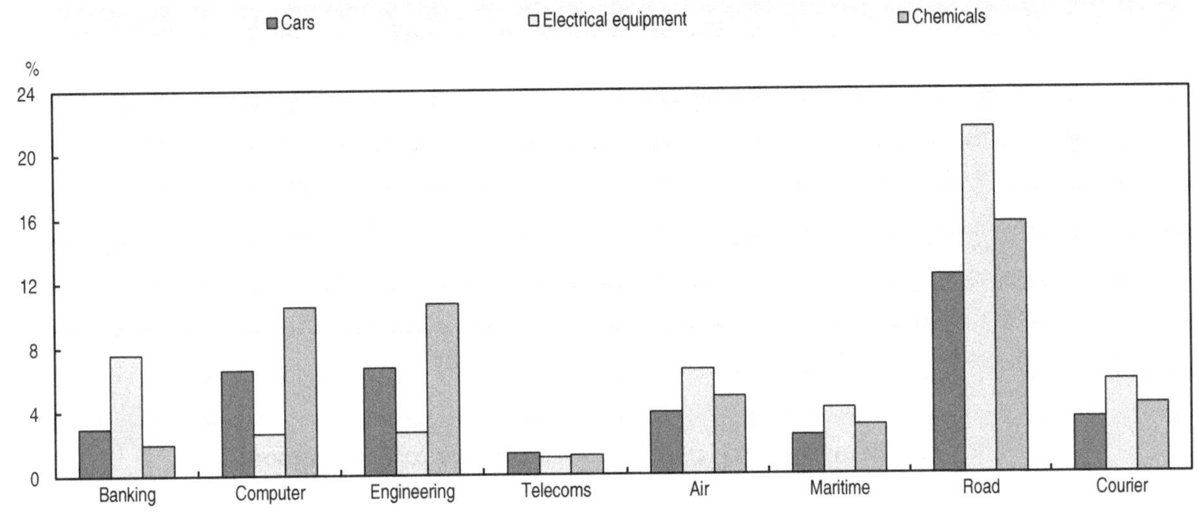

Note: The methodology is based on Arbache et al. (2016). Best-practice STRI means the country with the lowest score for the sector in the sample.
Source: OECD calculations based on the CEPII BACI database, 2014 data.

In the same manner, access to credit on competitive conditions is a prerequisite if firms are to compete in international markets. Open markets encourage widespread access to bank funding and compressed interest rate spreads, which in turn help firms get financing for innovation, working capital and trade. Where the regulatory environment is conducive to trade and FDI in commercial banking, manufacturing exporters in industries that rely on external finance perform better, entering more markets and developing more products for overseas customers. For instance, reforming the regulatory environment in commercial banking so as to halve the distance from the most liberal market could, for the average country, boost exports of electrical machinery by almost 8%, and automobile exports by about 3% (Figure 3.13). Intermediate inputs in fragmented global supply chains are more sensitive to financial conditions than are final goods, and exports in volatile industries such as fast fashion, and to countries with higher commercial and political risks, also depend critically on well-developed and well-functioning credit markets at home.

Knowledge-intensive services like software, communication services and R&D add value to products and processes. Fast transmission of information across production locations, efficient systems to monitor markets and to adjust supply continuously to customer tastes, computer-assisted design and manufacturing, and cutting-edge product development are all vital determinants of competitiveness in high-tech products. Innovative sectors are less successful on export markets when the regulatory environment limits competitive pressure at home in computer services, telecommunications and engineering. Under such conditions, R&D-intensive industries such as chemicals and transport equipment tend to export lower volumes, with sales thinly spread across markets in a more homogeneous set of varieties.

Policies with respect to services influence manufacturing export performance mainly because services help reduce production and transaction costs. For example, best-practice regulation supporting open and efficient transport, IT and finance is associated with more competitive export prices in downstream sectors, particularly so in final goods. Conversely, where essential services are not available at the best price due to regulation, the more expensive input costs and less efficient production processes tend to be reflected in less competitive export prices, which limit firms' ability to penetrate foreign markets.

Competitive telecommunications, in particular broadband internet, play a particularly decisive role in supporting quality improvements and vertical differentiation. Best-practice regulation in the sector is associated with a higher unit-value of manufacturing exports, suggesting that they are value-adding services which contribute to tilt exports towards the higher end of the market. This can be explained by the positive effect of pro-competitive regulation on the deployment of high-speed internet services, which provide firms with real-time tools to track and match ever shifting consumer preferences and to access information and innovation. Furthermore, internet services open up new possibilities to command a premium by bundling goods and services, including after-sales services, establishing customer communities on social media and the like.

Box 3.4. **Bringing services from a bottleneck to a springboard for manufacturing in Brazil and India**

India and Brazil are two emerging markets which have promoted the development of a stronger manufacturing base as prime policy priorities, through recent initiatives such as "Make in India" or *Plano Brasil Maior*. Detailed analysis of the experience of these economies highlights how upgrading services, including through better regulation, can be critical for the successful emergence of high-end industries. Improving the physical and virtual connectivity on which manufacturing supply chains rely is particularly stressed.

Brazil has established a solid comparative advantage in natural resources sectors, and its exports have largely relied on the strong competitiveness achieved in commodities. Brazil's manufacturing faces the challenge of diversifying and upgrading its export base. Less than 0.5% of all formal-sector firms sell abroad; the top 10 products account for 45% of total goods exports, and the share of high-tech exports has been falling over time. Export diversification would be strongly boosted by improving services that reduce production and trade costs, and that are currently underperforming, in particular finance, transport and logistics services. Brazil's top manufacturing exports, such as food products and iron and steel products, do not rely heavily on external credit, but industries targeted as priorities for development (automobiles, semi-conductors and medical equipment) require effective credit intermediation to grow. Some products like food and petroleum products benefit from Brazil's strength in natural resources to remain internationally competitive despite the high cost of transport, but improvements in supply chain infrastructure may be a necessary condition for sustainable expansion in the chemicals and automobile parts industries. Brazil would then be in a favourable position to leverage its highly-performing engineering sector to further develop innovative industries.

> **Box 3.4. Bringing services from a bottleneck to a springboard for manufacturing in Brazil and India** (*cont.*)
>
> In contrast to Brazil, India's exports in priority sectors (automobile and components, chemicals, electrical machinery, pharmaceuticals and apparel) already exhibit an advanced degree of diversification across products and markets, but they are thinly distributed and face challenges in scaling-up. Indian manufacturers also obtain export prices that are 6-15% lower than average in these products, indicating that they remain confined to low-end segments of the global market. To address the constraints on quality competitiveness and to scale up existing exports, analysis shows that a lack of high-speed internet services is creating a major bottleneck, especially regarding exports to high-income economies like the Unites States and the European Union, which are India's primary customers. While Indian consumers and businesses enjoy a vibrant and competitive market for mobile telecommunications, the country lags a long way behind the world average broadband penetration and access to secure servers. Pro-competitive regulatory reforms to improve fixed broadband services could significantly help extend the reach of Indian industrial businesses.
>
> *Source:* Arbache et al. (2016); Benz et al. (2017).

Well-designed regulatory systems make markets more attractive for foreign direct investment

In addition to the welfare cost of services trade and investment barriers to consumers and businesses, they also reduce the attractiveness of a market for foreign direct investment. Not only are tight regulatory environments less appealing for multinational enterprises (MNEs), but even those foreign multinationals that are able to absorb higher entry costs and succeed in establishing an affiliate in more restrictive markets have to face disproportionately high operational costs, which jeopardise their contribution to knowledge diffusion and value creation in the host economy.

Firms establishing abroad may face outright discriminatory regulations, such as nationality requirements for board of directors and managers, restrictions to the recruitment on foreign highly qualified personnel, prohibition from hiring locally licensed professionals, limited access to government contracts, and so on. All these factors increase their operational expenses. Multinational companies also bear higher compliance costs when facing new, unfamiliar and often different regulatory frameworks in every new market they enter. Consequently, countries seeking to improve their attractiveness for foreign investment could consider easing trade and investment barriers through unilateral or negotiated liberalisation, but also pursuing efforts to align aspects of their domestic regulation with regulatory environments observed in more open and FDi-engiendly economies.

Foreign investment provides a number of benefits to the host country, by acting on economic, social and political levers. Multinational companies create job opportunities by recruiting local employees. Furthermore, multinational activity is often associated with skill and technology transfers. Foreign affiliates may employ more advanced production techniques that can be diffused to the domestic economy, thereby contributing both to the skill upgrading of local workforce and to increased innovation incentives in the whole industry. The host country could also benefit from a wider choice of services products, of better quality and, under favourable regulatory conditions, at more attractive prices than local or imported substitutes.

Finally, multinational companies tend to expand their activities well beyond the geographical boundaries of the host country, hence contributing to boosting the host country's own exporting activity. Foreign affiliates act to a notable extent as export platforms, in particular supplying financial, transport, computer and distribution services not only to their local host markets but also to third countries (Box 3.5).

Box 3.5. **FDI-export platforms: The case of US and Japanese affiliates**

One of the channels linking FDI attractiveness and trade performance is the FDI export platform phenomenon. In this operating model, MNEs establish affiliates abroad not only to supply services to local customers, but also to serve as regional hubs or as specialised service centres for their corporate group in neighbouring markets.

Foreign affiliates of US services MNEs are largely set up to serve their host countries, with on average more than 70% of their total sales addressing local demand (Figure 3.14). However, foreign affiliates of US non-services parents are more strongly engaged in exports and intra-firm trade, which together comprise more than half of their total activity. This suggests that foreign services subsidiaries of US manufacturing MNEs are in large part established to support the production of the parent company or to reach out to further markets, acting as distribution hubs.

Figure 3.14. **Decomposition of total foreign affiliate sales, by final destination**

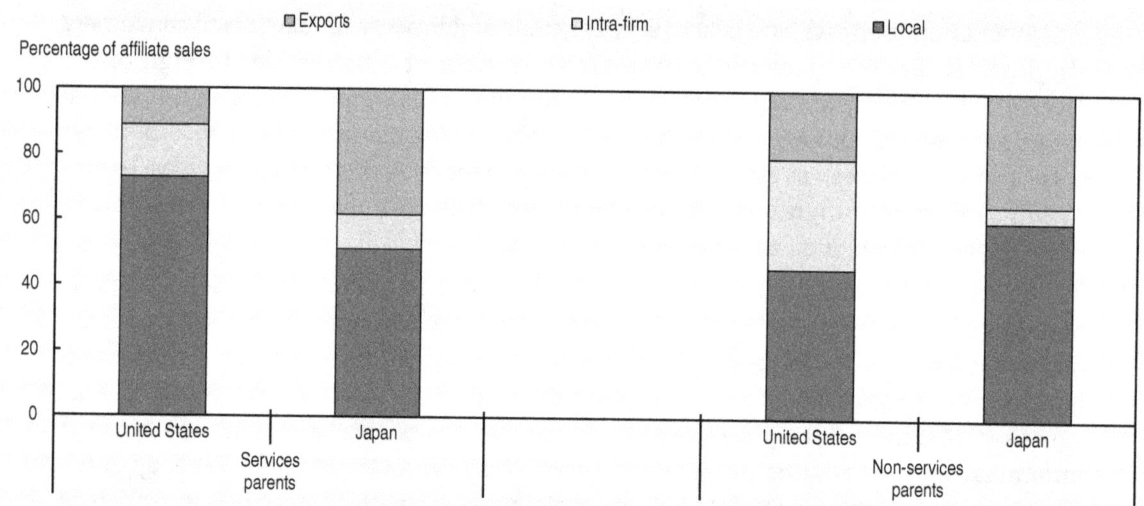

Note: The shares show respectively the percentage of sales of foreign affiliates that are destined to the local markets (local), to the parent firm (intra-firm) and to third countries or to unrelated parties in the home country (exports). Average shares across sectors over the periods: 2008-12 for the United States and 2008-13 for Japan.
Source: OECD calculations based on data from the US Bureau of Economic Analysis and the Japanese Ministry of Economy, Trade and Industry.

Similarly, the activity of Japanese foreign affiliates directed back to the headquarters or to third markets ranges between 40% and 50% of total foreign affiliate sales, depending on the main activity of the parent company. Hence Japanese MNEs, regardless of their core activity, appear to follow a strategy of establishing regional bridgeheads to sell more broadly than in their host market.

Nevertheless, the purpose of establishing foreign services affiliates differs considerably across sectors (Figure 3.15). In sectors such as construction, logistics and telecommunications, Japanese foreign affiliates are established mainly to achieve a better penetration of the domestic market. However, in some other sectors Japanese MNEs establish affiliates abroad not just to address local demand but especially to act as

Box 3.5. **FDI-export platforms: The case of US and Japanese affiliates** *(cont.)*

a springboard for exports. This export-platform phenomenon is most prevalent in finance and transport services. In transport, exports back to the headquarters account for almost one fourth of total affiliate sales. Together with exports to third countries, they represent over 70% of affiliate sales. In financial services, exports to third countries command two thirds of foreign affiliate sales.

Figure 3.15. **Decomposition of Japanese total foreign affiliate sales, by sector, 2008-13**

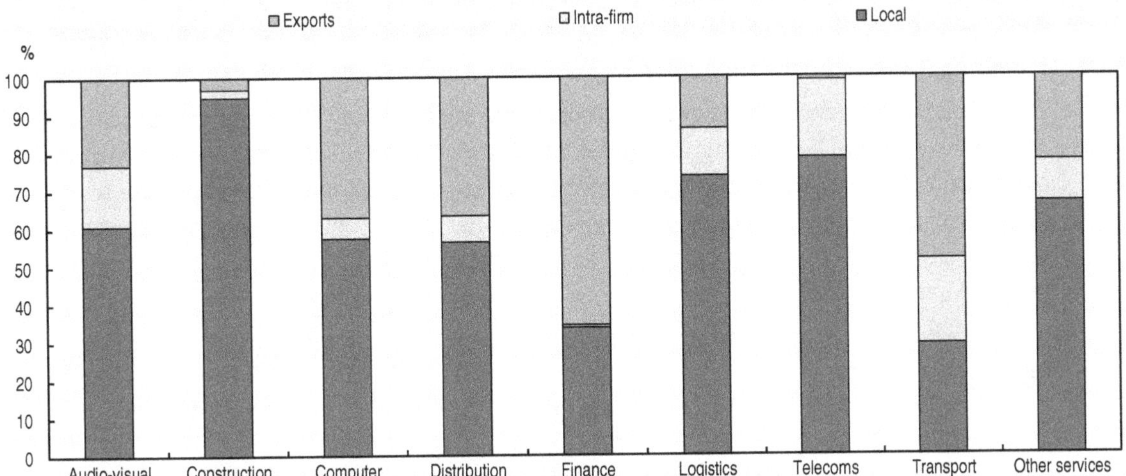

Note: The shares represent the percentage of sales of Japanese foreign affiliates that are destined to the local markets (local), back to the parent firm (intra-firm) and to third countries or unrelated parties in the home country (exports).
Source: OECD calculations based on data from the Japanese Ministry of Economy, Trade and Industry.

Export-platform sales are also relevant in computer and distribution services, with 37% and 38% of affiliate sales respectively. This evidence indicates that Japanese MNEs tend to develop a web of local establishments abroad to expand their client base both locally and in neighbouring countries, but also as providers of support functions to sustain the activity of the corporate group.

Services trade liberalisation boosts the competitiveness of the domestic economy

Open services are essential elements of domestic competitiveness and productivity growth. This section has highlighted the two main channels through which open markets bring wider benefits to the economy. Services trade liberalisation has the potential to boost a country's export performance by attracting foreign investment. Foreign firms bring about further advantages for the host market, in the form of new job opportunities, and skill and technology transfers.

Moreover, reducing services trade restrictions is also likely to influence exports by enhancing the competitiveness of existing firms both in services and in downstream manufacturing. New entrants push local services providers to become more efficient and more innovative in order to preserve their market shares. In becoming more productive, domestic firms can be encouraged to venture into new foreign markets. At the same time, the least competitive and inefficient companies might also be driven out of the market once they are no longer sheltered by protectionist measures. While this may require costly adjustments in the short run, it has the potential to unlock a far more efficient reallocation of resources towards high-performing firms with strong growth prospects.

Implications for trade policy-making

This chapter has examined the magnitude, nature and impact of the costs entailed by restrictive services trade policies. The new evidence provided is meant to inform trade policy makers about the likely effects of unilateral or concerted regulatory reforms and help prioritise policy action. Among the main implications emerging from the analysis are that:

- The existing stock of services restrictions has a clear dampening effect on cross-border trade and foreign investment activity. There is substantial scope for reducing trade costs in major services sectors by scaling back discriminatory measures towards foreign providers, but even larger gains would occur if more general domestic regulation regarding competition and transparency were concurrently improved.

- As explicit trade barriers come down, the costs of having to comply with different regulations in each jurisdiction become more significant for internationalised firms. There is ample opportunity for regulatory cooperation to make doing business easier for exporters while preserving adequate consumer protection and other public policy objectives. However, where high explicit restrictions to services trade still prevail, it is essential for them to be reduced before regulatory cooperation can make a substantial difference.

- Smaller and less experienced exporters face a heavier cost burden in more restrictive regulatory environments. Yet more and more often, small and young firms need to seek opportunities abroad to deal with stagnant domestic demand and rising scale economies in the digital world. Opening up services markets would primarily benefit SMEs, which are responsible for the greater part of new job creation.

- The business models for supplying services are complex, often involving a combination of modes, a bundle of goods and services, or a mix of digital products and face-to-face interaction. Where possible, policies should avoid, distorting those business models, specifically by adopting a balanced approach towards the different modes of supply through trade, investment and competition policies.

- There is not one service industry, but many services with different business models, competition challenges and best-practice regulatory frameworks. To maximise the benefits from reforms, targeted policy advice needs to identify the main bottlenecks by taking into account the level of preventable trade costs in each sector, how far sectoral regulation diverges from that of key trade partners as well as flow-on effects on downstream segments of the economy.

- Reforming services brings benefits for consumers but also strengthens productivity and performance in the domestic economy. Under competitive pressure, services firms are pushed to innovate and offer the most cost-effective solutions to their customers. Modern manufacturing is a heavy user of services inputs and its competitiveness relies on access to state-of-the-art suppliers at the best price. Countries with more favourable and transparent regulatory environments are also more attractive for FDI, stimulating economic activity, jobs and exports.

- The benefits of services trade liberalisation are, however, unlikely to come without temporary disruptions to labour markets. For gains from trade to materialise, some firms need to close down while better performing ones expand. Reforms towards more competition in services therefore work best for society if accompanied by effective safety-nets and active labour market policies. Such policies should be designed to mitigate the short-term effects on workers who may be displaced, to enhance their opportunities to find new jobs, and to make it more attractive and less risky to start new ventures.

Notes

1. This chapter builds on the findings of Arbache et al. (2016), Benz (2017), Benz et al. (2017), Miroudot and Pertel (2015), Nordås (2016), Nordås and Rouzet (2015), Rouzet et al. (2016), and Rouzet and Spinelli (2016).

2. The time period covered by the STRI and of the available trade and investment data precludes the identification of trade costs from policy changes within countries over time. Estimates presented in this chapter are derived from cross-country differences in policies, and are therefore better suited to represent the long-run potential of regulatory reforms.

3. The average STRI in the sectors considered is 0.29 for courier services, 0.24 for commercial banking, 0.23 for telecommunications and 0.23 for construction.

4. In other sectors, data are insufficient to conduct an analysis with satisfactory robustness or the resulting coefficients are not significant. Statistical uncertainty and the lack of precise information on the sensitivity of import demand to price changes mean that only a range of trade cost estimates can be reported.

5. These results are based on confidential firm-level data that cover foreign affiliates of corporate parent companies in Finland, Germany, Japan and the United States.

6. The average STRI in the sectors considered is 0.30 for transport services, 0.23 for computer services, 0.23 for telecommunications, 0.19 for distribution, 0.23 for financial services, and 0.23 for construction.

7. The discussion in this subsection is based on Miroudot and Cadestin (2017). The concept of value shops and value networks was first introduced by Stabell and Fjelstad (1998).

8. These estimates describe the average level of trade costs across all sectors and may hide significant variation at the sector level. Hence, it may well be that trade costs due to regulatory differences are substantially higher in some sectors.

9. There are two ways through which trade restrictions raise prices: barriers to entry create rents for existing firms, which can charge higher prices as long as they are shielded from competition from imports and from the potential entry of new suppliers; and excessive regulation increases the cost of compliance for established firms, which can be passed on in higher prices. Either way, these restrictions bring about a cost that is similar to a *sales tax* on consumers and downstream companies.

References

Arbache, J., D. Rouzet and F. Spinelli (2016), "The role of services for economic performance in Brazil", *OECD Trade Policy Papers*, No. 193, OECD Publishing, Paris, *http://dx.doi.org/10.1787/5jlpl4nx0ptc-en*.

Benz, S. (2017), "Services trade costs: Tariff equivalents of services trade restrictions using gravity estimation", *OECD Trade Policy Papers*, No. 200, OECD Publishing, Paris, *http://dx.doi.org/10.1787/dc607ce6-en*.

Benz, S., A. Khanna and H. Nordås (2017), "Services and performance of the Indian economy: Analysis and policy options", *OECD Trade Policy Papers*, No. 196, OECD Publishing, Paris, *http://dx.doi.org/10.1787/9259fd54-en*.

Lodefalk, M. and H.K. Nordås (2017), "Trading firms and trading costs in services: The case of Sweden", Örebro University, *School of Business Working Paper* (forthcoming).

Miroudot, S. and C. Cadestin (2017), "Services in global value chains: From inputs to value-creating activities", *OECD Trade Policy Papers*, No. 197, OECD Publishing, Paris, *http://dx.doi.org/10.1787/465f0d8b-en*.

Miroudot, S. and K. Pertel (2015), "Water in the GATS: Methodology and results", *OECD Trade Policy Papers*, No. 185, OECD Publishing, Paris, *http://dx.doi.org/10.1787/5jrs6k35nnf1-en*.

Nordås, H. (2016), "Services Trade Restrictiveness Index (STRI): The trade effect of regulatory differences", *OECD Trade Policy Papers*, No. 189, OECD Publishing, Paris, *http://dx.doi.org/10.1787/5jlz9z022plp-en*.

Nordås, H. and D. Rouzet (2015), "The impact of services trade restrictiveness on trade flows: First estimates", *OECD Trade Policy Papers*, No. 178, OECD Publishing, Paris, *http://dx.doi.org/10.1787/5js6ds9b6kjb-en*.

OECD-WTO (2017), "Trade in value added", *OECD-WTO: Statistics on trade in value added* (database), *http://dx.doi.org/10.1787/data-00648-en*.

Rouzet, D., S. Benz and F. Spinelli (2017), "Trading firms and trading costs in services", *OECD Trade Policy Papers*, forthcoming.

Rouzet, D. and F. Spinelli (2016), "Services trade restrictiveness, mark-ups and competition", *OECD Trade Policy Papers*, No. 194, OECD Publishing, Paris, *http://dx.doi.org/10.1787/5jln7dlm3931-en*.

Stabell, C. and Ø. Fjeldstad (1998), "Configuring value for competitive advantage: On chains, shops, and networks", *Strategic Management Journal*, Vol. 19, pp. 413-437.

Chapter 4

Services trade and policy supports inclusive growth

Chapter 4 provides a policy-oriented overview of the main findings set out in previous chapters, providing targeted recommendations on how co-ordinated government-wide strategies to improve services trade policies and regulatory frameworks can support inclusive economic growth, competitiveness, productivity and employment.

The ongoing structural transformation towards a services economy, across all countries and at all levels of development, has immense potential to improve well-being. This book synthesises the recent work of the OECD Trade and Agriculture Directorate to analyse services trade policies and to quantify their impacts on trade in goods and services, the performance of the goods and services sectors in the global economy, and how services trade restrictions influence the decisions and outcomes of firms engaged in international markets.

The complexity and dynamism of commercial activity in the 21st century has engendered a myriad of interlinkages across services sectors and the economy as a whole. Telecommunications, audio-visual and computer services constitute a digital network of services at the heart of the world trading system. Transportation, courier, logistics and distribution services form the backbone of global supply chains. Legal, accounting, insurance and banking services are essential enablers of trade and finance. Architectural, engineering and construction services are a fundamental foundation of physical infrastructure. Often, trade and regulatory policy in these individual services sectors are made with limited regard for economy-wide impacts.

In this context, the policy conclusions described below, and in preceding chapters, support the recommendation that national governments consider adopting whole-of-government strategies to capitalise on the demonstrated potential of co-ordinated services trade policy and regulatory reforms. The OECD Services Trade Restrictiveness Index (STRI), database and online policy tools provide comprehensive and comparable data and benchmarks relative to global best practices that can facilitate such efforts.

Open service markets are the gateway to global value chains

Open and well-regulated services markets ensure access to information, skills, technology, funding and markets in a modern, increasingly digital economy. For example, intermediate services inputs provide essential links in value chains. They move parts and components to the assembly line and final products to the end users; they design, engineer and innovate; they monitor demand and consumer tastes, and transmit such information to the product developers; they provide funding and insurance; and they facilitate compliance with laws and regulations in all the markets where the product is sold, to mention but a few functions. Depending on the position in the value chain, intermediate services help reduce costs, improve quality and match suppliers and customers around the world, as indicated in Figure 4.1.

Just as relative abundance of skilled labour is the basis for comparative advantage in skill-intensive sectors, a rich services supplier base forms the foundation for comparative advantage in services-intensive industries. The most services-intensive sectors also tend to be high-technology sectors. Moving up the value chain, therefore, depends on the presence of a local business services sector that is open to ideas, skills and investment from cutting edge firms wherever they may be found.

Figure 4.1. **Services in value chains**

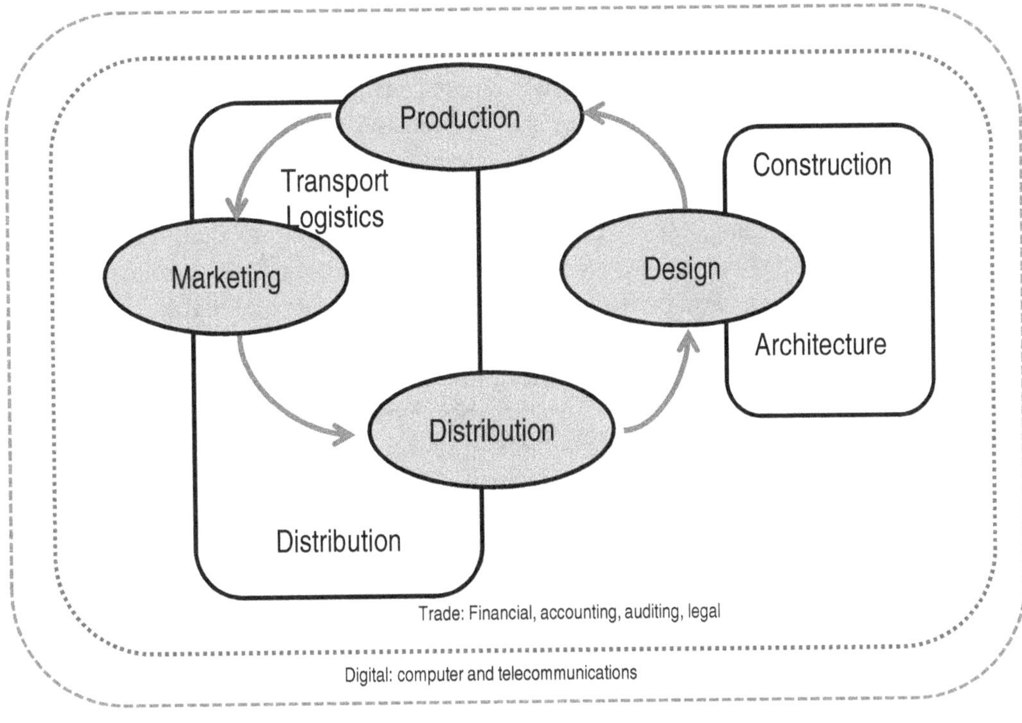

A competitive distribution sector is an important channel whereby firms, including SMEs, reach consumers. Reforms in this sector, particularly in emerging and developing countries, could help stimulate entrepreneurship in a host of goods-producing sectors including agriculture, and in addition benefit consumers.

Services reforms boost SMEs

Regulatory restrictions to services trade disproportionately discourage small firms and newer firms without export experience from competing in a market. These findings suggest that barriers to trade in services entrench the market shares not only of domestic firms, but even of large incumbent exporters. Deeper pockets, in-house legal expertise, broader existing networks of business partners at home and abroad, and the benefits of scale to absorb overhead costs are many reasons why larger firms are better equipped to succeed in complex and challenging regulatory environments.

Further evidence of this is the observation that the costs of services trade restrictions are generally lower for foreign-owned firms when exporting back to the home country of their multinational parent. This suggests that familiarity with the regulatory requirements of a market gives a decisive head start in dealing with restrictions, and that improving transparency would be a beneficial step towards reducing the costs associated with burdensome services regulations.

There are enough examples of services SMEs entering global markets, being "born global", to inspire and to initiate policy responses to promote such activities. Nevertheless, the broad picture reveals that global SMEs are relatively rare. Most services-exporting firms, regardless of size, export sporadically to one or a few countries and most export relationships last for only a year or two. The lack of persistence of SMEs in international markets suggests that complying with regulation in unfamiliar markets, cultures and languages may overwhelm them.

The high rate of sporadic exports suggests that the difficulty with exports may not be so much the entry into foreign markets as establishing a customer base there. The root of the problem seems to be a declining rate of start-ups in the local economy in most OECD countries combined with obstacles to gaining scale in foreign markets. This raises complex policy issues for governments that aim to reconcile high standards of safety and consumer protection with encouraging SMEs to take benefit of the opportunities that technology and trade liberalisation have created for entering international markets. A significant rate of failure is inevitable when taking risks in an uncertain environment. Therefore, markets for venture capital are needed and any government program supporting SMEs' internationalisation must deal with failures as a normal part of taking risks rather than as a failure of the program. Having said that, governments also need to identify the market failure as well as the policy options to address market distortions and evaluate the costs and benefits of taking action.

It is clear that the cost of services trade restrictions falls disproportionally on SMEs because of the high fixed-cost component. Therefore, lowering the regulatory burden where feasible would be more effective in making globalisation work for all. In addition, regulatory cooperation to minimise duplication of compliance costs and better use of technology to ease the burden of administrative procedures would also help SMEs. Exports are not an objective in itself, but in cases where opportunities in the home market are small they may represent an attractive strategy for successful start-ups to expand and gain scale quickly.

Regulatory co-operation reduces trade frictions

Regulatory heterogeneity has a negative impact on services trade flows, over and above the impact of services trade restrictions. Conversely, countries trade more with partners that have similar regulation. The trade effect of regulatory heterogeneity is higher the less trade restrictive the countries are: harmonising at a low level of restrictiveness is associated with a large boost to services trade, whereas harmonising at higher levels of restrictions would not produce any benefits. Trade agreements are likely to have the largest effect on trade when i) the parties are relatively similar in terms of approaches to regulation and the regulatory framework, ii) the first step is to reduce the level of trade restrictiveness, iii) reducing the level of restrictions goes hand in hand with forward-looking regulatory cooperation, iv) regulatory cooperation becomes more prominent as the level of trade-restricting regulations comes down, and v) regulatory cooperation successfully eliminates duplication of regulatory compliance costs for exporters.

Movement of people is part of trade in services and trade agreements

Movement of people may not account for a large share of services trade, but it is still essential for international business operations. Mobility of natural persons across international borders is crucial, particularly for trade in business services, which in turn is an important channel for knowledge transfer. In addition, OECD analysis shows that restrictions on the movement of people are negatively associated with foreign affiliate sales.

To attract foreign services multinationals, countries need to liberalise rules governing the movement of people for the purpose of providing a service on a temporary basis. Business travel could be facilitated through effective and inexpensive visa processing facilities such as electronic visas. Flexible arrangements such as temporary licensing of professionals for specific tasks or shorter time periods would also help in areas where licenses are needed. International trade agreements like the General Agreement on Trade in Services (GATS) have provisions for the movement of natural persons providing services, as a category distinct from migrants and job seekers. Few countries make that distinction in the migration laws and regulation, however.

The digital economy depends on services, and brings new services to global markets

Telecommunications are not only crucial for the co-ordination and synchronisation of manufacturing supply chains. Broadband also constitutes the infrastructure that makes knowledge-intensive business services tradeable, facilitating knowledge transfers across borders. OECD analysis shows that liberalisation and pro-competitive reforms in the telecommunications sector are associated with a substantial reduction in the trade costs for business services. Furthermore, the services that gain the most from access to better and less costly telecommunications networks are specialised, high-end or customised services.

High-capacity networks at competitive prices are a necessary but not sufficient condition for a digital transformation of knowledge-intensive services. Access to the professions and the services they provide is also essential. Licensing by self-regulated bodies creates entry barriers, limits supply and raises prices of the regulated professions. Furthermore, since qualification requirements differ across countries, states and territories, mutual recognition agreements can be complex to negotiate and even more difficult to enforce. The recent agreement between the European Union and Canada (CETA), for example, includes a framework for regulatory bodies to negotiate mutual recognition agreements for professions that are "regulated in each Party, including in all or some Member States of the European Union and in all or some provinces and territories of Canada [article 11.2]". Thus, despite the existence of a comprehensive trade agreement, there are still potential hurdles to overcome before professionals can provide their services across the CETA membership.

Digitisation and standardisation of tasks are rapidly eating into the reserved areas of licenced professionals. To ensure that manufacturers and SMEs everywhere have access to knowledge-intensive professional services, there is a need to review which activities need to be licensed, whether licencing could be vested with an independent body, and deepening international regulatory co-operation. Examples of such co-operation are international accounting standards and the APEC agreement recognising "substantial equivalence" of professional competence in engineering. For the market for knowledge-intensive services to function properly, professionals must be allowed to deploy staff to their clients as needed and to accumulate, transfer, store and analyse data to help clients in the most cost-effective way.

Open and well-regulated services markets support inclusive growth

A deeper understanding of the role of services trade and policy in national economies and the global trading system is particularly important at a time of uncertainty regarding the role of globalisation and technology in the context of growing income and wealth inequality. Widening income inequality is to a larger or lesser degree observed universally, but countries differ substantially in their ability to make growth inclusive.

In the long run, the main source of economic growth is technological progress. The ongoing ICT technology revolution goes hand in hand with openness to trade, investment, information and ideas, and one would not be possible without the other. Thus, technological development and globalisation are two sides of the same coin. Technological development relies on global access to knowledge and to the networks, goods and services that carry the knowledge around the world. Furthermore, the scale that open markets offer often enhances the returns to innovation. Conversely, technology has brought down trade and transaction costs substantially, in many cases more than the liberalisation of policy-induced barriers to trade.

The ICT technology/globalisation nexus, like technological revolutions before it spurs on new business models and products. In this context, education reforms are essential for better matching of workers with jobs. Adult education and training, as well as giving more space for entrepreneurship training in vocational education, are important elements of such reforms (OECD, 2016). Finally, well-designed basic safety nets such as health, pensions and unemployment insurance improve labour mobility and encourage entrepreneurship. With such safety nets in place, restructuring of firms, changing jobs and starting a business all become more attractive and less risky.

References

OECD (2013), "OECD guidelines on the protection of privacy and transborder flows of personal data", *www.oecd.org/sti/ieconomy/oecdguidelinesontheprotectionofprivacyandtransborderflowsofpersonaldata.htm.*

OECD (2016), *Skills matter: Further results from the survey of adult skills*, OECD Skills Studies, OECD Publishing, Paris, *www.oecd.org/skills/piaac/skills-matter-9789264258051-en.htm.*

ANNEX

STRI indices by sector

The digital network

Figure A.1. **Telecommunications services, 2016**

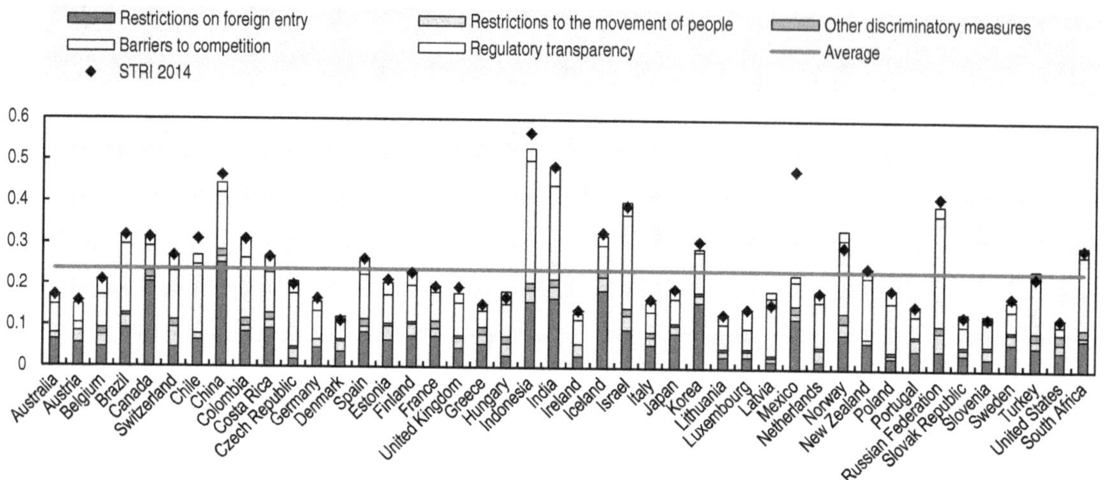

Figure A.2. **Television and broadcasting services, 2016**

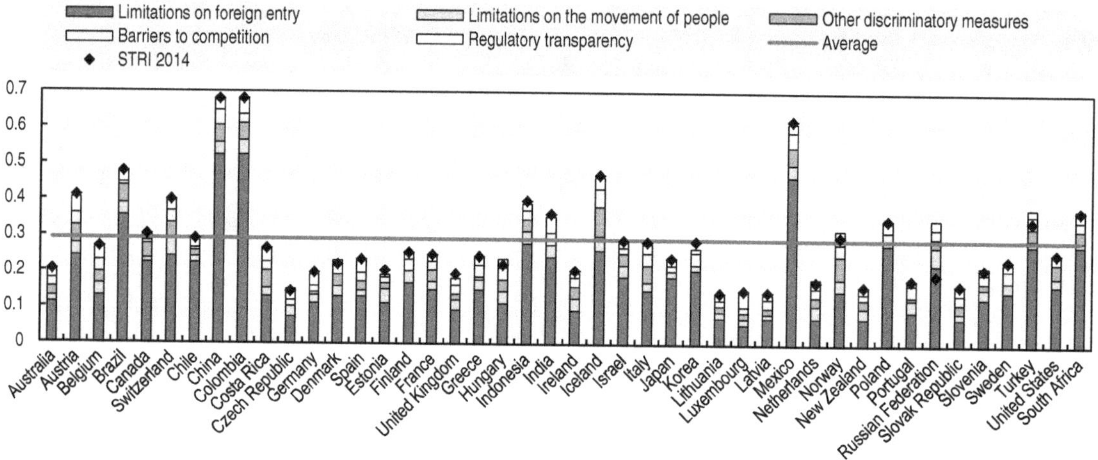

Figure A.3. **Motion pictures services, 2016**

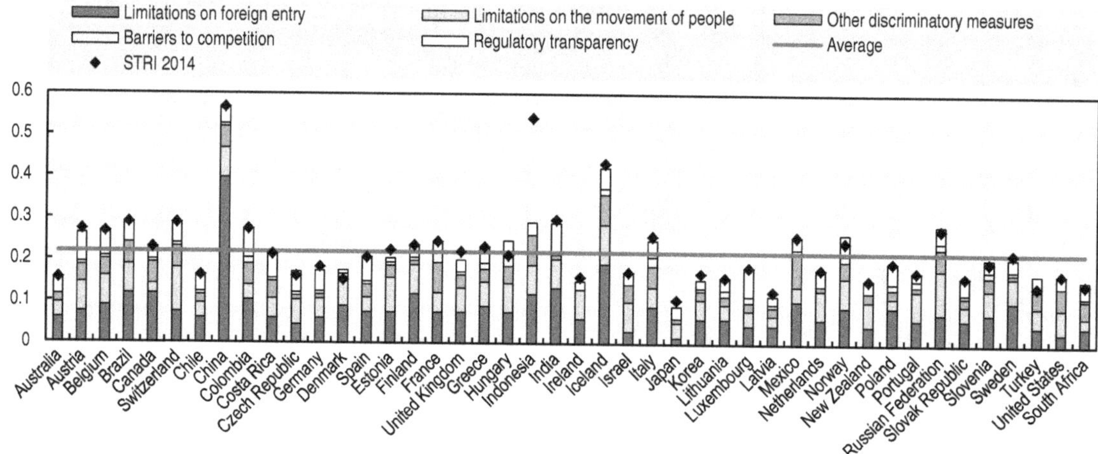

Figure A.4. **Sound recording services, 2016**

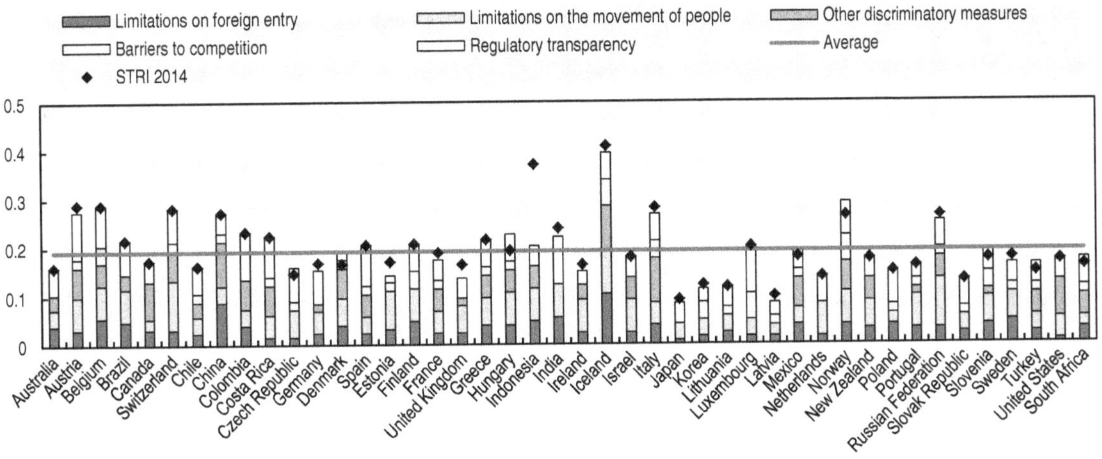

Figure A.5. **Computer services, 2016**

The transport and distribution supply chain

Figure A.6. **Air transport services, 2016**

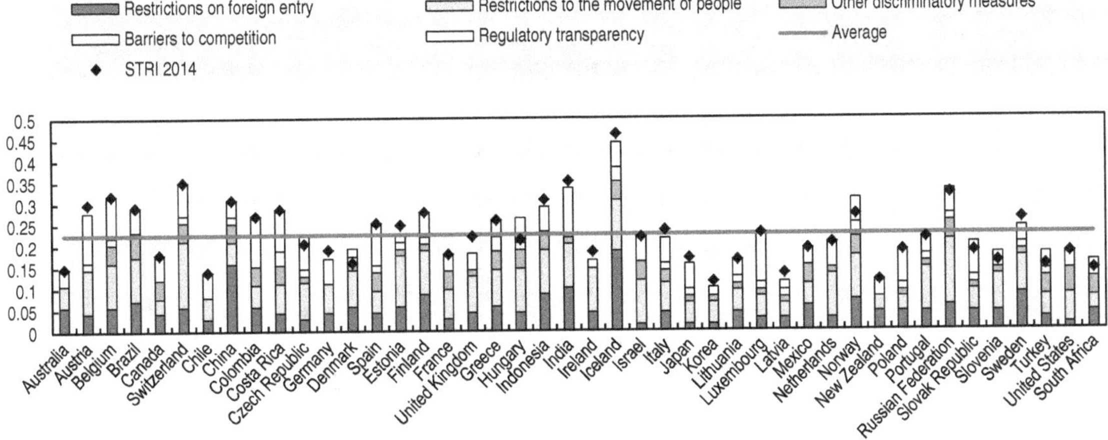

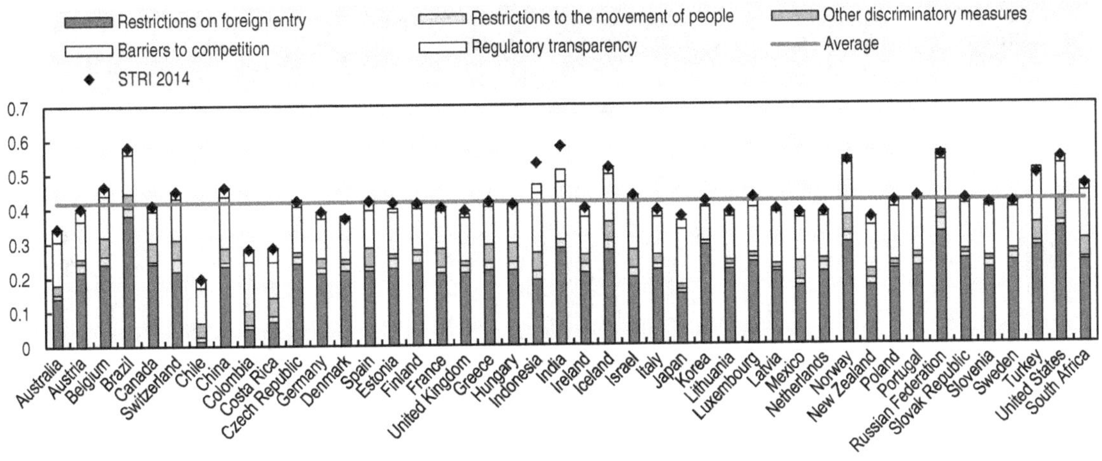

Figure A.7. **Maritime transport services, 2016**

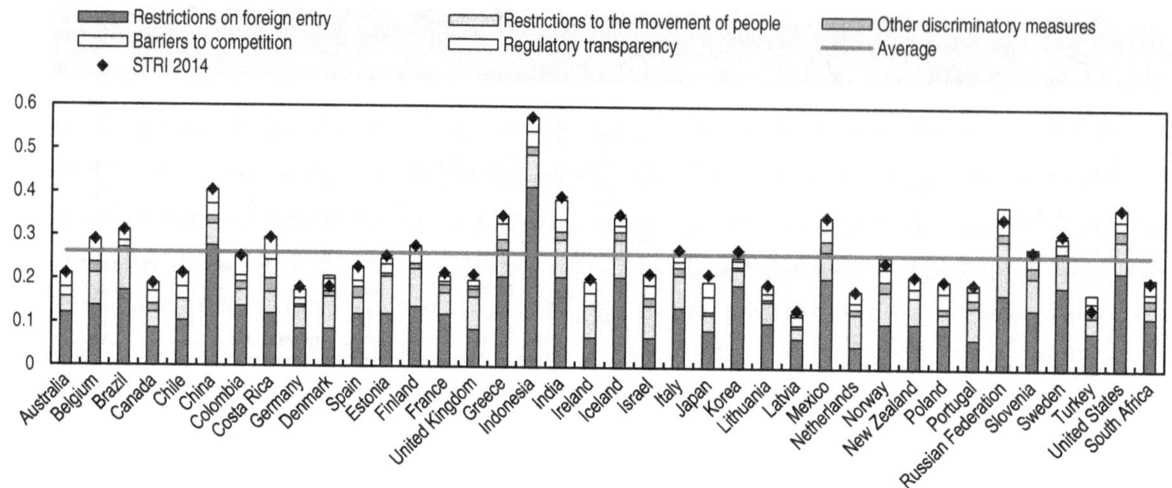

Figure A.8. **Rail freight transport services, 2016**

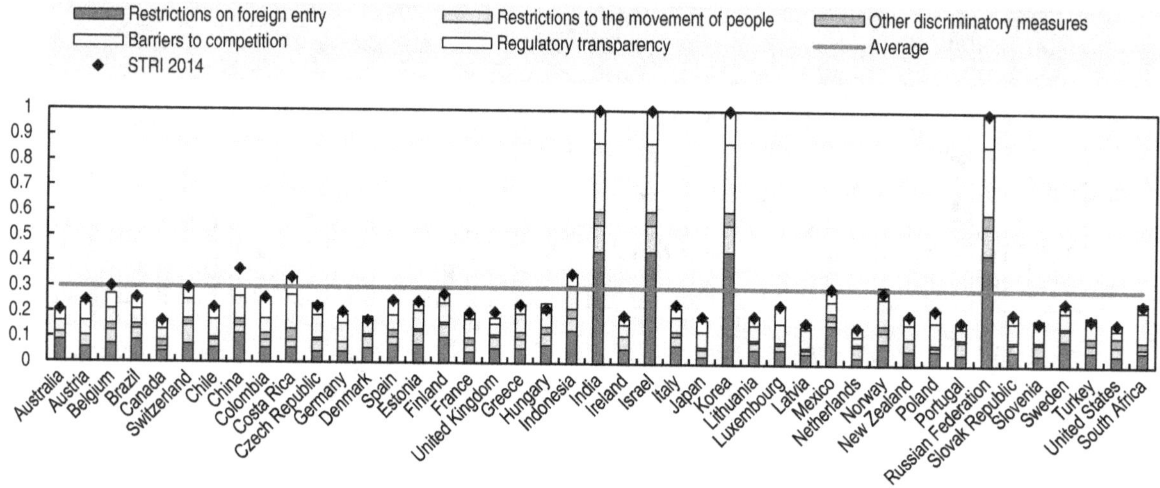

Figure A.9. **Road freight transport services, 2016**

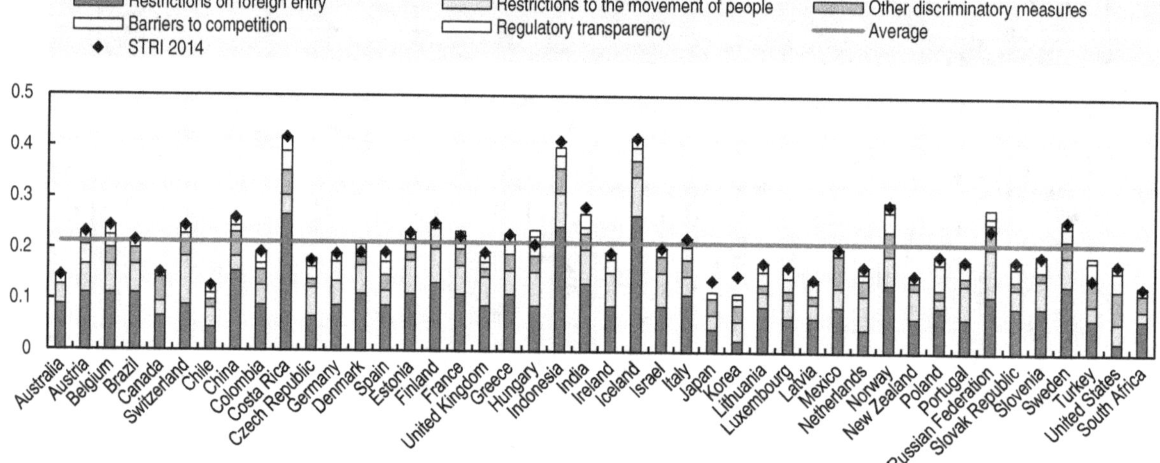

Figure A.10. **Courier services, 2016**

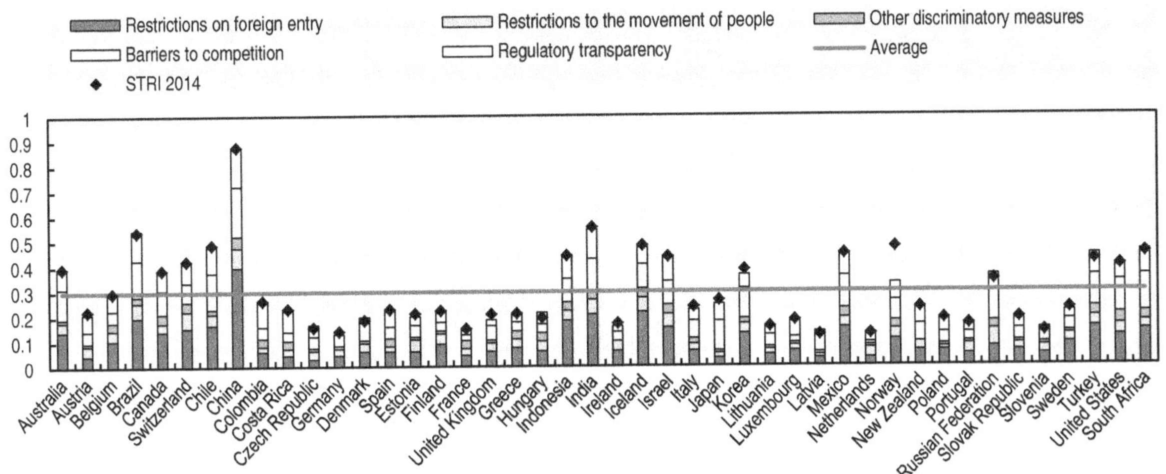

Figure A.11. **Distribution services, 2016**

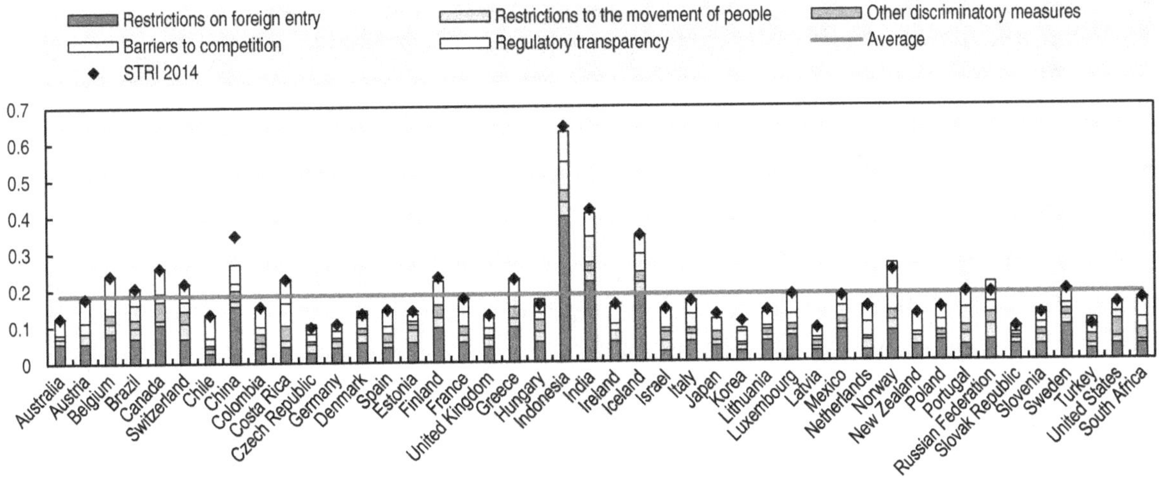

Figure A.12. **Logistics cargo-handling services, 2016**

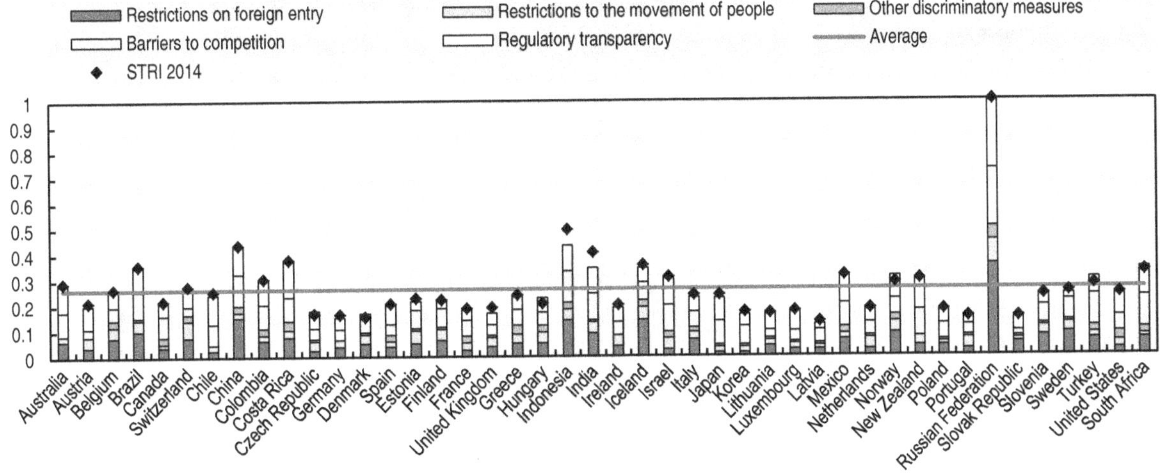

Figure A.13. **Logistics storage and warehouse services, 2016**

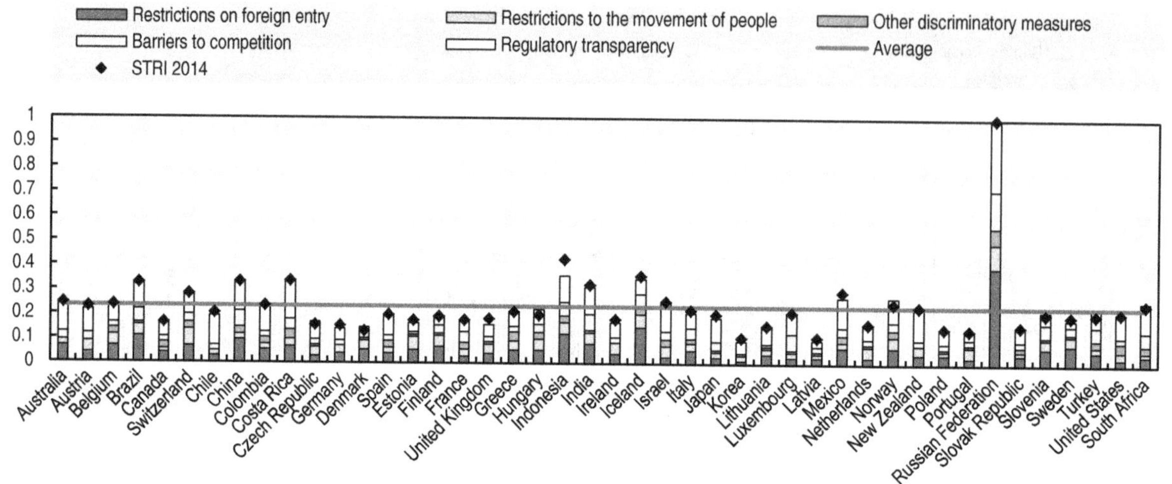

Figure A.14. **Logistics freight-forwarding services, 2016**

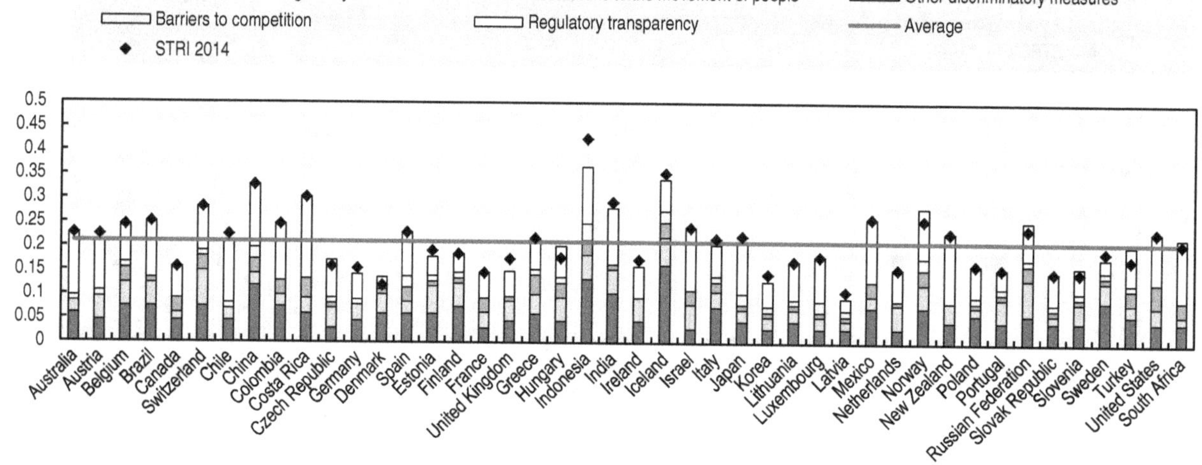

Figure A.15. **Logistics customs brokerage services, 2016**

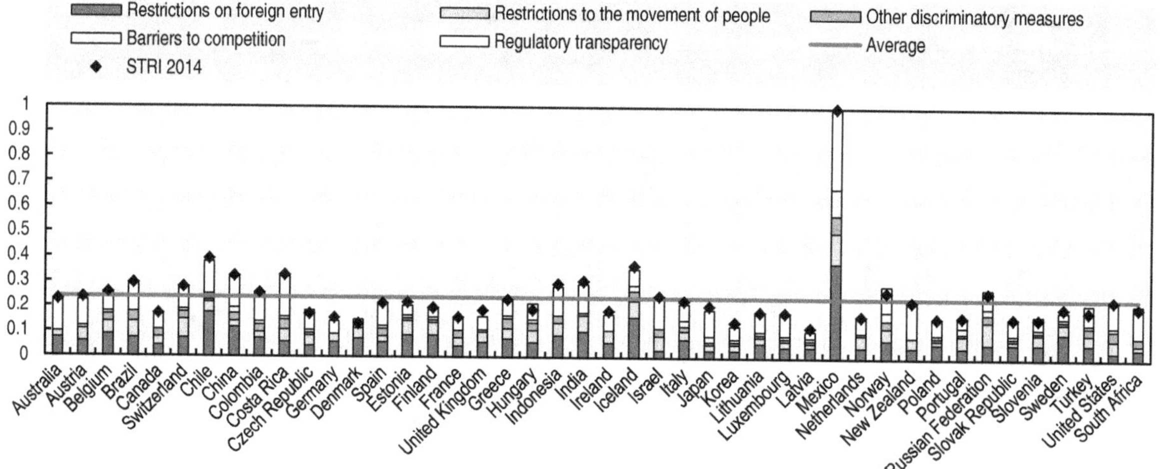

Market bridging and supporting services

Figure A.16. **Commercial banking services, 2016**

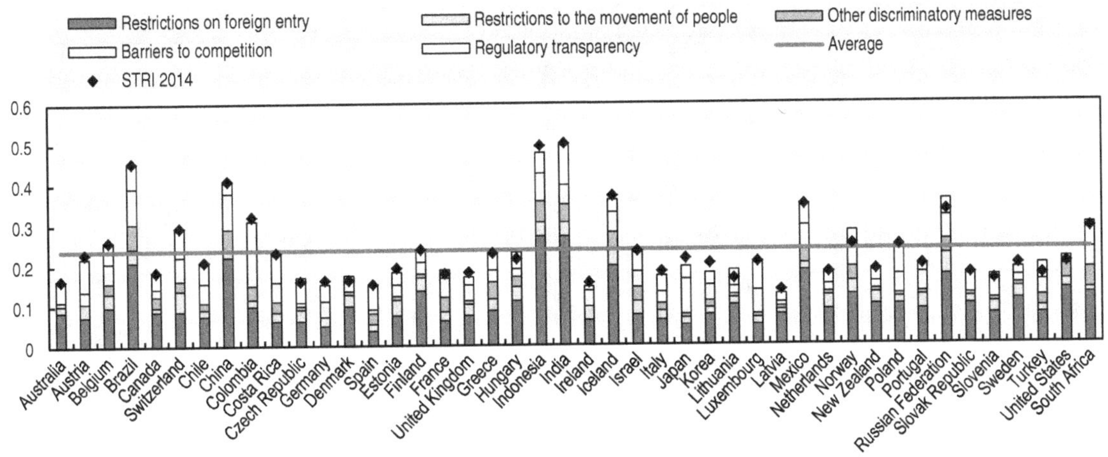

Figure A.17. **Insurance services, 2016**

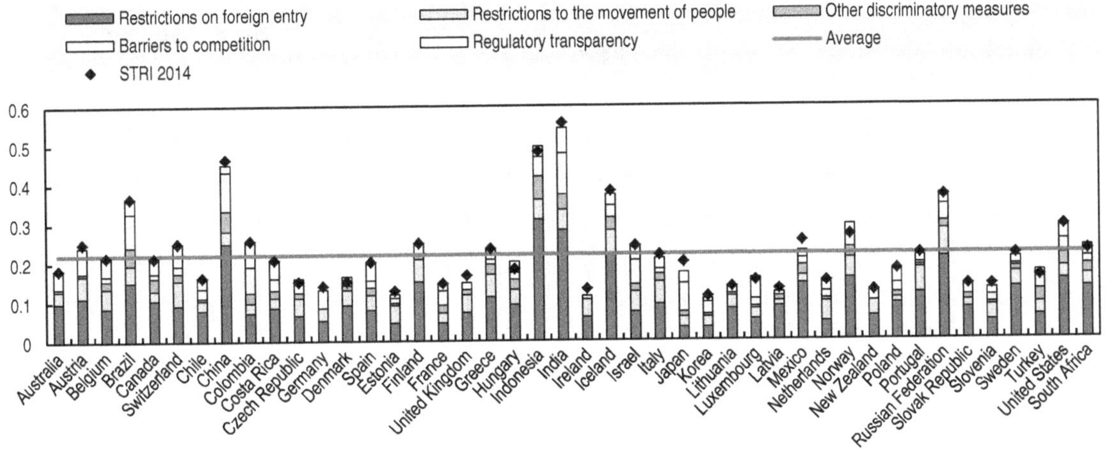

Figure A.18. **Legal services, 2016**

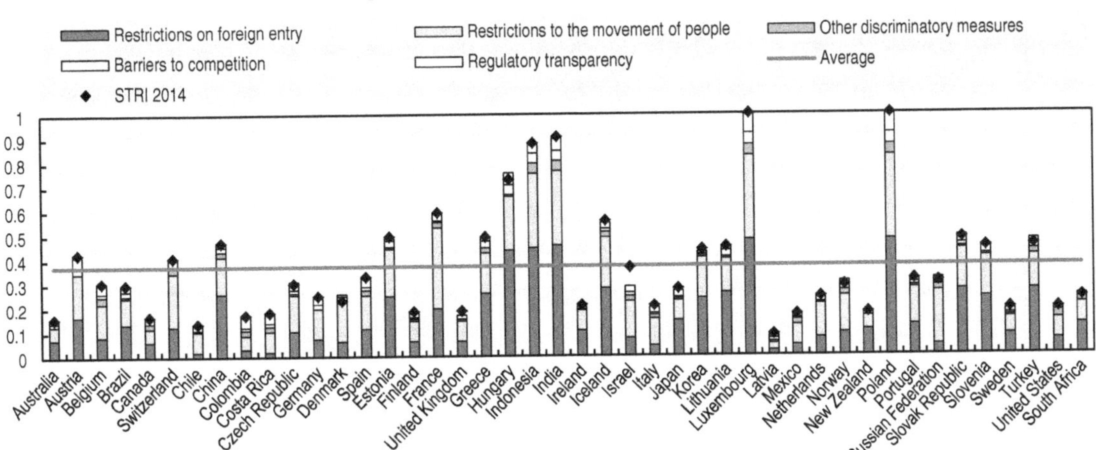

Figure A.19. **Accounting and auditing services, 2016**

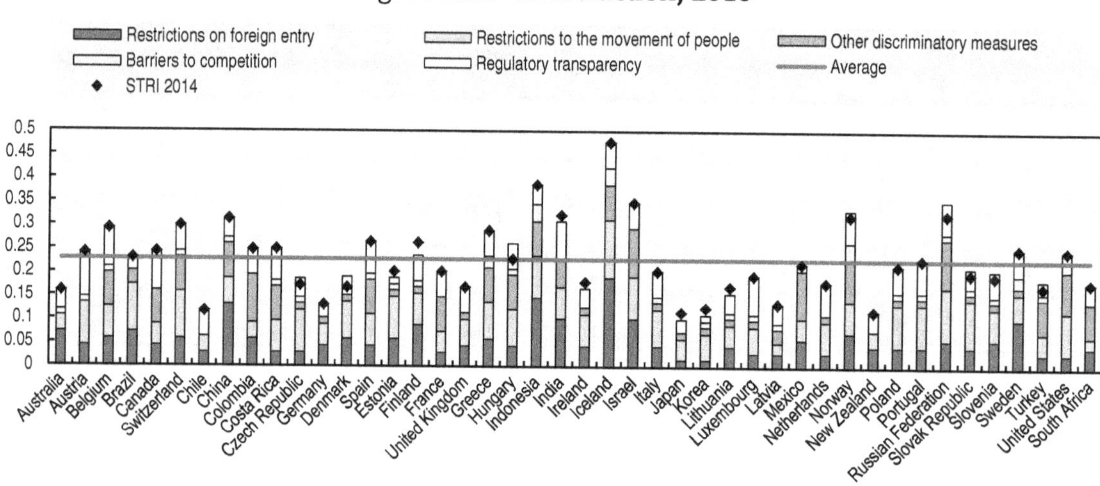

Physical infrastructure services

Figure A.20. **Construction, 2016**

Figure A.21. **Architecture services, 2016**

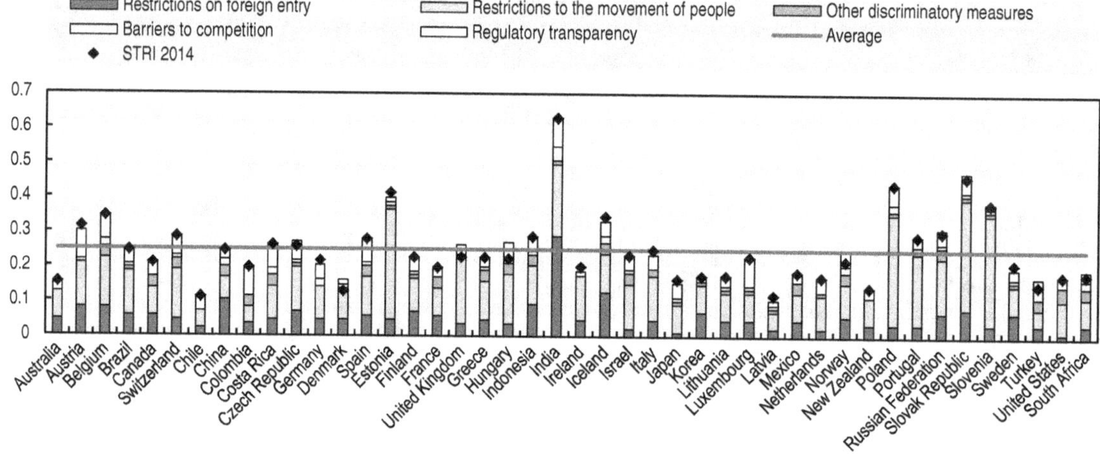

Figure A.22. **Engineering services, 2016**

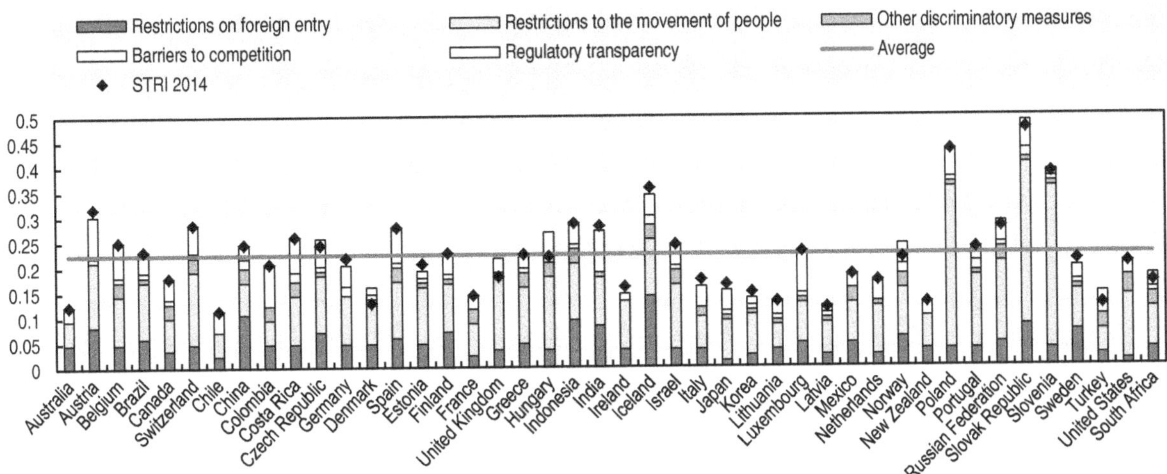

ORGANISATION FOR ECONOMIC CO-OPERATION AND DEVELOPMENT

The OECD is a unique forum where governments work together to address the economic, social and environmental challenges of globalisation. The OECD is also at the forefront of efforts to understand and to help governments respond to new developments and concerns, such as corporate governance, the information economy and the challenges of an ageing population. The Organisation provides a setting where governments can compare policy experiences, seek answers to common problems, identify good practice and work to co-ordinate domestic and international policies.

The OECD member countries are: Australia, Austria, Belgium, Canada, Chile, the Czech Republic, Denmark, Estonia, Finland, France, Germany, Greece, Hungary, Iceland, Ireland, Israel, Italy, Japan, Korea, Latvia, Luxembourg, Mexico, the Netherlands, New Zealand, Norway, Poland, Portugal, the Slovak Republic, Slovenia, Spain, Sweden, Switzerland, Turkey, the United Kingdom and the United States. The European Union takes part in the work of the OECD.

OECD Publishing disseminates widely the results of the Organisation's statistics gathering and research on economic, social and environmental issues, as well as the conventions, guidelines and standards agreed by its members.

OECD PUBLISHING, 2, rue André-Pascal, 75775 PARIS CEDEX 16
(22 2017 01 1 P) ISBN 978-92-64-27492-1 – 2017

www.ingramcontent.com/pod-product-compliance
Lightning Source LLC
Chambersburg PA
CBHW081840250726
48659CB00008B/2531